SOUL RE
FOR THE
DRY AND WEARY
CHRISTIAN

CATCH

THE

RAIN

CORELLA ROBERTS

All Scripture quotations, unless otherwise indicated, are taken from the Holy Bible, New International Version®, NIV®. Copyright ©1973, 1978, 1984, 2011 by Biblica, Inc.™ Used by permission of Zondervan. All rights reserved worldwide. www.zondervan.com The "NIV" and "New International Version" are trademarks registered in the United States Patent and Trademark Office by Biblica, Inc.™

This is a work of nonfiction; however, many of the names have been changed to protect the privacy of the people in the narrative.

Book Layout © 2017 BookDesignTemplates.com

Cover design: miblart

Catch the Rain/ Corella Roberts. -- 1st ed.
ISBN 978-1-7346853-1-2

Dedicated to Greg and Corinne,
who reintroduced me to myself and the Lover of my soul,
and to Brent and Julie, who demonstrated how to stay in
love with Him.

CONTENTS

Endorsements

With the tender-hearted wisdom of someone intimately familiar with the wilderness, Corella offers both her own vulnerable stories as well as practical soul-work advice. For those who are feeling dry and empty, her gentle and steady words will point you to the One who overflows with love and longs to fill every cracked, weary heart.

—**Sarah Hilkemann**, Velvet Ashes Program Director

Corella Roberts, missionary teacher, wife, and mother of three, knows well how life's stress and busyness can lead to burnout. In *Catch the Rain*, Corella offers us a vulnerable peek into her own journey from spiritual dryness and burnout into a deep and refreshing relationship with the God who truly loves us and longs for us to rest in his love. *Catch the Rain* is worth reading simply for the enjoyment of witnessing the author's journey into greater freedom and joy. But through the reflection responses at the end of each chapter, Corella also offers us a treasure trove of questions and practices that can help us, too, draw nearer to God and experience his tender and passionate love more deeply. If you find yourself weary and dry, you will find this lovely book a trustworthy guide, leading you back to the heart of the God who loves you and longs to draw you close.

—**Dr. Carolyn J. Watts**, spiritual director and author
of *Risking Rest*

Catch the Rain is a beautiful companion for the thirsty soul. Corella uses God's love story throughout scripture as well as her own story to invite the reader to journey with God through all the seasons of the heart. At the end of each chapter Corella has included well thought questions and spiritual practices to help the reader experience God's love in the midst of where you are in your own story. You'll want to read this book slowly and with a journal. Whether you are weary, burned out, or simply looking for a guide to help you pay attention to the desires of your heart and to the love of our Father, you'll find *Catch the Rain* to be a helpful companion for the journey.

—**Frances Green**, Spiritual Director and Member
Care Provider for Barnabas International

I read *Catch the Rain* in a season of the Lord drawing me deeper into His love, a love I thought I had experienced but realized while reading this book just how much more He has to show me! He really met me in these pages.

—**Kala**, mom, missionary, Jesus-follower

Come, let us return to the Lord.
He has torn us to pieces
    but he will heal us;
he has injured us
    but he will bind up our wounds.

After two days he will revive us;
    on the third day he will restore us,
    that we may live in his presence.

Let us acknowledge the Lord;
    let us press on to acknowledge him.
As surely as the sun rises,
    he will appear;
he will come to us like the winter rains,
    like the spring rains that water the earth.

— Hosea 6:1–3

Introduction

GROWING UP IN THE PACIFIC NORTHWEST, I had no real understanding of a dry season. Fall rains turned into winter snows turned into spring runoff turned into summer thundershowers. Some years, August crackled with dry pine needles and wildfires, but it never seemed to last too long.

Then, nine years ago, I moved to Northern Thailand. Fifty percent of our year is spent sweating in the humidity and battling mold, but when the rains stop, they stop. The lush tropical foliage turns brown from both thirst and dust, and when it catches fire, little can be done to control it.

On top of this oppressive, dry heat, the rice farmers burn their fields, and our beautiful valley becomes an ashtray. On the worst days, black soot flutters from the sky and we hide indoors, wearing air filtration masks if we venture out into the hazardous air. We pray, watch for any sign of clouds, and pray some more until the rains return after two to three months of smoke.

Before all this, I didn't understand what it meant to literally ache for rain. At least not in a physical sense. My soul, however, knew this kind of parched land all too well.

CATCH THE RAIN

My husband and I, eager to step into our calling as missionary teachers, jumped out of college and into a school in rural Alaska. Teaching and serving there proved beyond difficult, and it drained me.[1] Two young children with beautiful but intense personalities, who thought sleep was for the birds, drained me. Being involved with nearly every possible school function drained me. Then, moving to the other side of the planet without a season of rest and debriefing drained me. Mostly, my performing and striving and keeping up the good Christian show drained me. My soul was emptied. Frazzled. Dry. Burned-out.

At that point, I discovered that one of two things can happen to the heart of man. The soul is needy;[2] it must be satisfied, and in its desperation, it will start consuming anything and everything indiscriminately. Relationships are sucked dry in this unhealthy thirst. Cravings are momentarily satiated with shots of pleasure. Deep pains are numbed, and broken dreams are ignored as the disconnect between the soul and God broadens.

That disconnect is the danger zone—it's where those leaders we admire seem to come suddenly crashing down. They kept up outward appearances while their inner worlds wasted away. The soul must be satisfied, and when it is dry, it can choose to drink the poison of the world.

Or…

This parched and weary soul can turn its feeble cry Godward. It can crawl onto the hot sand of its desert, lay itself bare to the cloudless sky, and cry for rain.

This is the story of my cry and of God's open-handed response. But more than that, it's an invitation for you to join me, and a guide to the practices that restored my soul, that taught me to love again, that introduced me to Jesus in a way I never would have understood before my desert.

God sees you—faithful pastor, do-it-all teacher, responsible ministry leader.

God hears you—worried parent, sacrificial missionary, dedicated servant to your church.

God holds you—fight-hard prayer warrior, the wearied caregiver, compassionate counselor.

Your labor is not in vain, but it is also not the sum of who you are. No matter how much you love your ministry, no matter how deeply you feel called to it, it is not the crux of your worth to your Father. And He did not give it to you so that it would destroy you.

God invites you to partner *with* Him, under His easy yoke, serving and loving out of an overflow of peace and joy. My prayer is that my words will be a companion as you shed the weight of all you're not meant to carry and find your way back to His embrace.

What I'm longing for you to know is that *your Father cares about the state of your soul.* The Good Shepherd longs to lead you to quiet waters. Green pastures. Soul restoration.[3] And if He wants this for you, it's okay to want it for yourself.

Please take the time you need to walk with Jesus through this book. Allow Him to guide you and gently correct you without rushing the process. Give your soul room to breathe.

This world, my friend, is a dry and weary land. We no longer live in Eden where "streams came up from the earth and watered the whole surface of the ground" and the very footsteps of the Lord God were heard "walking in the garden in the cool of the day."[4]

Rather, we live as strangers and aliens in this land that is groaning for Christ to return and make it all new. We're waiting for the final garden, where God will dwell with men again, wiping away our tears and quenching our life-long thirst from the spring of living water.[5]

Until then, we must catch every precious raindrop.

Only by the grace of God can I write these words to you. Only because he called to me in my wilderness and allowed me to see my sin can I echo his whisper to your heart:

Come, all you who are thirsty,
*   come to the waters;*
and you who have no money,
*   come, buy and eat!*
Come, buy wine and milk
*   without money and without cost.*

Why spend money on what is not bread,
and your labor on what does not satisfy?
Listen, listen to me, and eat what is good,
and you will delight in the richest of fare. (Isaiah 55:1–2)

Here we are, Lord, desperately dry without you. Won't you teach us to catch the rain?

Part 1
A DRY AND WEARY LAND

If you ask people who don't believe in God why they don't, the number one reason will be suffering. If you ask people who believe in God when they grew most spiritually, the number one answer will be suffering.

— John Ortberg, *Soul Keeping*[1]

KEY STEP:
LEARN TO LISTEN

Throughout Part One, I'll offer my thoughts and experiences on paying attention to both the state of your soul and the voice of God. One significant practice to guide you through this section is the *examen*.

The daily practice of *examen*[2], as originally developed by Ignatius of Loyola, includes five basic steps:

1. Become aware of God's presence
2. Review the day with gratitude
3. Reflect on your emotions and actions; confess any sin
4. Pray about an aspect of your day
5. Seek wisdom and hope for tomorrow

However, as with any spiritual practice, it's more about the goal of drawing near to Christ and so becoming more like Him than it is about how we do it. I invite you to modify the above steps to facilitate your own growth best.

I also invite you to *do* this practice as you read this section.

Warning Signs

I SWEPT THE SMALL PAPER scraps off the low table into the garbage can, but one fluttered away on a whim of its own. Stooping to pick it up off the floor, I bumped the table, sending metal feet skidding along the tile with a shriek that echoed around the concrete room. I muttered something unrepeatable and glanced at my two-year-old daughter who was practicing her pincer grasp on a paper shard of her own.

Grabbing it from her before she could shred it further, I turned on my mom-voice. "Thanks for helping clean up! Such a big girl."

My husband opened the door and peered in with his usual grin. "How was Sunday school today?"

I shrugged. "Okay." There was more I could say about the kid that didn't speak any English, the quarrel that ensued between the twins, the knot in my back from attempting to hold a fussy toddler while simultaneously helping kids with the craft, or the terrible markers that were all dried up from lids that wouldn't stay on because nothing ever works properly in this unbelievably hot country!

But I didn't.

"I need to find some paper towels to wipe the glue off the tables. Mind taking her?" I pointed to our golden-haired toddler on the floor.

"I can get you something to wipe the tables!" And with that, he bounded away.

But. . . but. . . I want out of this room! I need a break. I need to be done. I need a new life!

Did I just think that?

Deep breath.

In pounced all the Christian self-talk: "Don't believe the lies." "Don't grow weary in doing good." "This may not feel like much, but God can still use it." "Give thanks." "Fix your gaze on Christ." "Consider others more highly than yourself." "Jesus loves the little children. . ."

Oh great, now that song's stuck in my head.

Troy returned with some dampened tissue paper. And not double-ply Kleenex, either. This was the typical Thai fare of tissue that disintegrates upon touch.

"Sorry. It's all I could find," he apologized.

I responded with a noise that sounded a bit like a cat hawking up a hairball.

Five minutes later, the glue had been somewhat smeared off the tables and we packed up the diaper bag, preparing to go home.

Troy bravely ventured a question, "Do you want to stay for lunch today? It looks like that egg stuff the kids like. Not spicy."

I shook my head. "I'm tired. I just want to go home."

He understood. Or, as a man of boundless energy, perhaps it's more accurate to say he accepted my weakness.

We found our five-year-old son out on the swings, and several minutes later we also found his shoes.

I just didn't know if I would ever find my joy again.

A sense of exhaustion that won't relent regardless of how much sleep you get; a ripple of frustration and anger that boils just underneath the surface most days; a lack of motivation to care for your body, your soul, or your relationships—escapist activities are far easier; and a loss of satisfaction in the activities that used to bring you joy. Those are a few of the indicators of burnout, or at least of the chronic stress that can lead to burnout.[1] Sound familiar?

I hope not, but the reality is that over 90% of people in ministry report having experienced some form of burnout.[2] It's an easy hill to slide down when you want to live wholeheartedly for Jesus. However, admitting to burnout is anything but easy.

After all, we know that carrying the cross of Christ is difficult. We feel called to bear one another's burdens. We recognize the reality of spiritual warfare and expect to face battles regularly. We know that obedience involves sacrifice. We've seen from the Father's example that unconditional love is painful.

11

These are scriptural truths, and many of us hold them as core values. Sometimes, however, there are other beliefs beneath them. Less truthful ideas. Guilt-inducers. Soul-crushing motives. As you read the following list, pay attention to which ones stir a reaction in you (agreement, defensiveness, sadness, guilt, or resistance, for example).

- I don't want God to be disappointed in me.
- He has entrusted me with this work, and it's up to me to hold it together.
- I'll lose the support of my church, my family, or my financial partners if I take a break from my ministry.
- No one else can do what I'm doing.
- Who am I without this role?
- God wants me to love through this hardship, even if it kills me.

If you've found something you want to sit with, write down for further examination, or talk to God about, please take a moment to do that. In fact, I encourage that to be your mode of reading and interacting with the Spirit throughout this entire book.

Western Christianity seems particularly prone to pushing its ministers to bear more responsibility than necessary. Our busy culture values productivity, balancing multiple roles, and a growing audience to prove growth. It's not preached from the pulpit, but it is quietly prevalent. And facing these unhealthy pressures and their subsequent motives in our lives will be countercultural, bringing resistance within and possibly without.

I have a vivid memory of a class I was taking in college—I think we were studying the Gospel of Mark—when the professor, who was also a local pastor, challenged us to consider how much time we were investing in kingdom-building activities. He paused his lecture, looking from one glassy-eyed face to another, and stated, "You all have more to give than you think you do." His jaw clenched. "Most people are just busy with the wrong things."

I sensed his anger, but I didn't understand until many years later that he was more than likely feeling alone in his responsibilities, disappointed in those who didn't care the way he did about the church, and frustrated with a group of Bible college students who, for the most part, probably put minimum effort into their class assignments.

As an impressionable nineteen-year-old, I heard his words as authoritative, almost threatening. I surely didn't want to become one of *those* people who under-gave to God.

This instance, along with many others, combined with my personality and pride to create a false motive that I still struggle with to this day: *The more I do for God, the more valuable I am to Him.*

That pastor was right, of course. Most of us *are* busy with the wrong things, but just because it's a church or ministry thing, is it a *right* thing? There are innumerable good works to be done in this sin-scarred world—orphans to be fed, homeless to be sheltered, uneducated to be taught, slaves to be freed, Bibles to be shared. Not to mention dishes to be washed, scraped knees to be kissed, trash to be picked up, painful stories to be heard.

Oh, Lord, we want to see Your kingdom come and Your will be done on earth as it is in heaven!

But I must first remember, it's *God's* kingdom, *God's* will, *God's* work, and *God's* responsibility. What a difference it makes to join Him in kingdom work rather than do it for Him! How can we hear His invitation and lean only on the strength of His spirit if we are constantly bombarded with guilt, false motives, and the expectations of others?

It all starts here, with learning to listen to our souls in the presence of Jesus. The very first step toward soul restoration is to dig deep with the Holy Spirit and find out what's going on in your heart. And He will lead you, oh so gently, to those quiet waters of refreshment and renewal.

You might feel bone-weary and dry, but don't worry, the thirsty landscape of your soul will serve to soak up even more of the outpouring of His love and grace that He longs to give you.

So, for now, simply open your hands. Close your eyes. Invite Jesus near. And just breathe.

Catch the Rain

Here you are invited to open your heart in the presence of Jesus. Please choose *1 or 2 reflection responses* that you are drawn to. You can take time for this. You are worth it.

 Keep a note of how many times over one week you long to say or do one thing, but feel compelled to be responsible, meet a need, or perform a certain way instead. (For example, *I have a headache and am totally exhausted, but I will lead Bible Study anyway.*)

Ask someone close to you if they sense that you're living out of weariness and diligence or out of abundance and overflow.

Make a list of ten things that bring you joy. How often are you doing each of those things? Now, make a list of ten things that drain you. How often are you doing those things?

Set a timer for two minutes and sit in complete, distraction-free silence. What came to the surface of your mind and emotions?

A Splintered Soul

YOU KNOW THOSE TIMES WHEN you're trying to wrap up a project and go home, but your coworker won't stop talking to you? Or you're scrambling to make dinner when your child has a potty accident on the floor? Or even when you're enjoying a great video on YouTube that's abruptly interrupted by an ad? Those are times of divided attention and they leave us feeling frustrated, impatient, and somehow robbed.

Dividedness of soul is similar. Your affections are all over the place. Your desires can't make up their mind. Your devotion keeps flitting away from Christ alone.

I find my own dividedness most easily during times of corporate worship. My lips are singing the words, but my mind is running through my to-do list. My hands are raised to exalt my God, but my heart is exalting myself. I'm horrified to admit this. There have been times I've had to just sit down in silence because I can't wrangle the attention of my wandering heart.

"Prone to wander, Lord I feel it. Prone to leave the God I love."[1] Yes, those are lyrics I can sing and fully mean.

As I write this, a late-April storm turns the city street below my café window perch into a slurry of rain and

17

scampering people. Scooters, common in Thailand, pull into the shelter of the overhang, their drivers dismounting into puddles and dashing around with various bags over their heads. Cars continue their journey with furiously beating wipers, otherwise unbothered by the deluge. In the median, flowering trees wave their purple frocked branches, beckoning for more life-giving rain.

I often long to be like a tree. Standing firm yet flexible in the storms. Doing precisely what I was designed to do, nothing more and nothing less. Accepting the seasons with grace, knowing that growth and fruitfulness will find me again come spring.

But perhaps you've seen trees in the opposite state—a fir consumed by beetles, a fruit tree withered from root rot, an oak split by lightning. Each silenced of production and stunted if not destroyed.

There are dangers to your soul within and without; your only safety and sure ground the all-consuming love of Christ.

You've begun already to pay attention to your inner world—your motives, responsibilities, joys and pains. Now, we invite the Spirit to continue the search, revealing sin and the wounds that often underly it. You may need to begin by asking Him to give you the desire for purity of heart. A longing for wholeness. An awakening to your weakness. Because sometimes, our outward façade is so strong that we even fool ourselves. A bit of holy undoing might be exactly what we need.

After a particularly exhausting and trying season, I found myself in close cahoots with my pet sin—craving attention and affirmation from men besides my husband. I confessed with tears and tried to shake it off, but months later I was still feeling the splintered pieces of my soul left in its wake. I had no idea where to begin healing. I didn't want to ever go down that road again, but I had the suspicion that I hadn't completely broken free from it yet.

It was there, in that desperately dry and brittle place, that the Lord gave me a prayer: *Give me an undivided heart that is fully satisfied in You alone.* For a while, I hardly spoke to God without first starting with this cry.

He also gave me the first step toward wholeness through fasting. I'd practiced the discipline of fasting from food occasionally before becoming pregnant, but very rarely after having children. It turned out that telling my flesh *no* was a great way for my spirit to say a bigger *yes* to God.

I appreciate how John Mark Comer points out that the often-forgotten practice of fasting encourages "life change through our *stomachs.* We're so used to books and podcasts and university lectures and teachings at church that we often forget: We're not just brains on legs. We're whole people ... so our apprenticeships to Jesus have to be whole-person endeavors."[2]

I was finally, for the first time in a long time, longing for God. I craved His satisfying presence through fasting and praying, and my splintered soul began mending enough to hold His healing rain again.

When I first started praying for an undivided heart, I didn't realize it was scriptural, but David wrote surprisingly similar words 3,000 years ago.

Teach me your way, Lord,
that I may rely on your faithfulness;
give me an undivided heart,
that I may fear your name. (Psalm 86:11)

This place of longing is the only place to start. We recognize our weakness and beg the Father to reorient our hearts. Our thoughts and desires might be scattered, splintered by years of striving, sacrifice, and self-deception, but He is calling us back. He wants nothing more than our complete reliance on His faithfulness. Our undivided devotion to His name.

Indeed, we are prone to wander, but hear the beautiful reminder from the final stanza that is usually omitted from "Come Thou Fount":

O that Day when freed from sinning,
I shall see thy lovely Face;
Clothed then in blood-washed Linnen
How I'll sing thy sovereign grace;
Come, my Lord, no longer tarry,
Take my ransom'd Soul away;

Send thine Angels now to carry
*Me to realms of endless Day.*³

One day, we will be fully and finally freed from sin and death, sorrow and sighing, fear and pain. Until then, we must continue to pray that God would "bind our wandering hearts" to His.

As you remove distractions from His love, pull out weeds of doubt, and collapse fully into God's grace, you'll be ready to start catching the rain. Because, if you know where to look, it's a downpour out there.

Catch the Rain

Here you are invited to open your heart in the presence of Jesus. Please choose *1 or 2 reflection responses* that you are drawn to. You can take time for this. You are worth it.

- Find a trusted friend and confess any blatant sin in your life, asking them to pray for your healing. Make restitution or get professional help if needed.

- Take note of the more socially acceptable sins in your life, such as neglecting proper care of your body, gossiping under the guise of prayer requests, boasting about your accomplishments as a form of testimony, or overworking to the point of ignoring your family. Ask God to help you uncover the wound beneath these. What does He say to you about it?

- Practice some form of fasting this week. You can fast from food, screens, producing, speaking, or even driving. Choose something that will give your spirit room to connect with God deeply.

- Write down a one-sentence prayer that you want to lean into right now. Place it somewhere you'll see often.

Ears to Hear

TROY AND I SAT HIP to hip on the swinging seat, sipping our Thai teas and watching the Chiang Mai traffic buzz by. This eclectic little coffee shop provided a unique late-night setting for a date on my birthday. Here we could talk, uninterrupted, while our kids slept back at the hotel and our friends in the room next door kept an ear to the baby monitor.

But what should we talk about? My default is to hash out details of life, plans for the coming weeks, hopes for the next season. Only on this night, I held a deeper conversation inside. One I was slightly nervous to broach.

I needed to share with him that God had spoken to me.

Not what I learned from the Word, not what I gleaned from a sermon, and not a blessing I received from a friend's prayer. I wanted to tell him what God had said to *me*. Only, this wasn't the norm in our spiritual conversations. In fact, we'd sat under more teaching than not that discouraged this kind of personal conversation with the Lord: How could you be sure it was God? You might misplace your trust in a word that is merely your own wishful thinking or, worse, a seed from the enemy.

It was better to play it safe, and just rely on the specific directives of the Bible. I was cautious there, too, though, not wanting to infer something personal that would misconstrue the original intent of the author or take a verse out of context. Yes, I'd clearly taken my college course on *Principles of Biblical Interpretation* to heart. And not that any of that is wrong. Not that people don't mishear God, misconstrue the Bible, and misinterpret the Spirit's leading. But...

In my zeal against false doctrine, I'd completely forgotten that God *does* want to communicate with me personally. I'd lost sight of the profound joy set before Jesus that allowed him to endure the cross[1]—the restoration of His bride and unity with His beloved.

I am His beloved.

You are His beloved.

What is a relationship with God without communication? I'll tell you what I think it is: religion. Dry, dutiful religion. And that's what I'd been operating out of for far too long. My mind and body followed Jesus, but my heart was far from Him.

Mark Batterson hits it on the head when he writes, "God will never lead us to do something that is contrary to His good, pleasing, and perfect will as revealed in Scripture. That said, Scripture doesn't reveal the logistics. That's the job of the Holy Spirit... although [scriptural] truth is timeless, it doesn't reveal now or later. Scripture gives us guidelines, but the Holy Spirit is our Guide."[2]

A month before this coffee shop conversation with my husband, I'd been invited to join a spiritual formation class. The idea seemed nice, but another after-school commitment felt exhausting. I was about to say "No thanks, I'm good" when my friend running the class approached me. She sincerely seemed convinced that I ought to come.

"Why should I join this class?" I challenged her.

Corinne didn't skip a beat as she replied, "My husband and I wouldn't still be here if we hadn't gone through it."

That was enough for me. I knew just enough of their story to know that they'd been through the wringer during their previous years in missions and that they seemed to be different after their sabbatical year in the States. If they felt it was that instrumental to their longevity in ministry, then clearly there was something there I hadn't studied before.

To my great surprise and delight, she was right. It wasn't so much something new for me to *learn* as it was something life-giving for me to *experience*. And one of the first premises that knocked me off my high horse of religious pride was this concept of listening to God.

"Hearing God cannot be a reliable and intelligible fact of life except when we see his speaking as one aspect of his presence with us, of his life in us. Only our communion with God provides the appropriate context for communications between us and him."[3]

27

I was discovering, or perhaps uncovering, the forgotten fundamentals of life in Christ, communion with God, and fellowship with the Holy Spirit. No amount of serving or Christian rightness would bring me there. I began to wonder if my desire to serve God well had driven me to become more of a Pharisee than a disciple. But now, a new way to follow Him emerged. A listening way. Beginning to hear the Master's voice like an eager child was the first step toward walking hand in hand with Him again.

My soul craved the life-giving nearness of my Savior.

"So, I'm trying to learn how to discern God's voice," I began, taking a sidewards glance at my husband's expression. He didn't seem shocked or concerned, so I continued, "and I think He said something to me the other day."

At this point, you're probably expecting me to reveal something the Lord said that altered the course of our lives or completely changed my perspective. But all that Jesus said to me at that time was a loving response to my praise. "Thank you, my daughter." While His words were sweetly simple, they rang loud and clear in my heart and felt incredibly profound, personal, and true. And, for the first time in several years, I allowed myself to say that God talked to me.

I'll let you decide whether or not that's a big deal.

As we walked back to the car, hand in hand, I felt a deeper sense of communion with my husband than I had in a long time, and I let his words wash over me and settle in those aching places of my heart. "I'm glad you're listening to God. Thanks for telling me."

Catch the Rain

Here you are invited to open your heart in the presence of Jesus. Please choose *1 or 2 reflection responses* that you are drawn to. You can take time for this. You are worth it.

- List all the ways you can think of that God speaks in scripture. (Try 1 Kings 19:9–13; Exodus 33:7–14; Mark 1:9–12, 35; Acts 10:1–20; Romans 1:18–21.)

- Journal about a time you discerned God's voice. How did you know it was Him?

- Spend some time in nature. What picture of His attributes does God reveal to you there?

- Ask God a question—something weighing on your heart—and listen for the answer as you go about your day. Be sure to record His reply and how you received it.

- Begin each morning with this prayer, "Speak, Lord, for your servant is listening" (1 Samuel 3:10).

Eyes to See

I STARED AT THE PAGE, my soul on paper. My relationships were clearly not meeting my expectations, and my loneliness was bigger than I cared to admit. Yet right next to these longings sat a list of thanks and an empty space waiting to be filled with God's response.

Twiddling my pen, I thought through my day. The puzzle pieces of my day began snapping into place as I invited God to give me His perspective. What had *I* done to be a good friend? Where did Jesus reach out to me? And did I grab His hand or push it away?

I jotted my memories and ended with a specific idea for taking initiative in my relationships, wrapped in a prayer for God's help and grace. I came to that page with the weight of loneliness, but I left with the joy of companionship—an awareness of a friend who sticks closer than a brother.

Shakespeare penned the famous quote that "all the world's a stage, and all the men and women merely players,"[1] and in many ways he's right. People will cross your life's stage during various scenes of peace and rest, trouble and sorrow. But no matter who plays the regular supporting roles, there are only two characters who are constant: you and God. Which begs the question, what did God do and say in the scenes of your day?

If you're not seeing Him, it's not because He isn't there.

It could be, though, that your spiritual eyes have forgotten where to look. Children are often better at seeing God throughout their day. We can learn from them how to be observant of and thankful for the most obscure things. The paper scrap that looks like a cat. The comfort of a parent's nearness. The play of emotion through music that they absolutely cannot resist wiggling their bodies to. The rivulets of water dancing their way down a car window on a rainy day.

Is it possible that God can be seen in every raindrop?

Our attunement to His active presence in our lives every day can be the difference between a life of abundant joy or mounting pain. It's one thing to believe God is with you, for you, and guiding you, but it's an entirely different experience to see *how* He is with you, for you, and guiding you.

The starting place for this practice is thanksgiving. The good old discipline of counting your blessings. *Eucharisteo*, as it's called in Greek.

Ann Voskamp writes, "Do I always want to see more beauty—more of the glory of God? Because that is what I am made for—to give Him more glory. More eucharisteo, more. And not only yesterday. But today—manna today or I starve."[2]

32

She beautifully notes the mysterious correlation between thanksgiving and spiritual food. The act of giving thanks is two-fold, one part magnifying the Giver of the gifts, the other part nourishing the soul of the gift's recipient. It's not only the gift itself that sustains us, but also the act of remembering it and attributing it to its source.

I see this at work in my human relationships, too. My husband cuts the grass, or my kids pick up their toys. That's great. I'm physically blessed by the outcome of their contributions to our home. But in pausing to verbally thank them, I'm both building them up and cementing their gift in my mind. The outcome of this? Stronger relationships.

That's what it all comes down to. What it will always come back to. Our relational connection with our Father.

Like a grateful child, we can look around our lives and realize that He has given us absolutely everything we have. Even what we think we purchased on our own was bought with the allowance He gave us. His fingerprints are all over every moment of our lives. His attention never turns away from us for a moment.

When you lift your face upward in thanks and adoration, you turn your eyes toward His smile. Then, with His face shining on you in your mind's eye, you have courage to examine the uglier parts of your day. The time you cursed at that terrible driver. The long line at the checkout that made you late to pick up your children. The projector that kept flicking off in the middle of your presentation.

33

The phone call from your best friend with news of a life shattering diagnosis.

Where was God in each of those moments? What was He saying? How did He invite you to notice Him?

He's not only with you in the shiny, happy experiences. He's with you in those painful ones, too. And even if you didn't notice Him at the time, He—the I AM outside of time—can take you back in your memories and show you how He was holding you and fighting for you.

This doesn't make all the bad and broken okay. It's not a way to gloss over the hard. Rather, it's a method of fully acknowledging the realities of your day, feeling them again in Abba's presence, and discovering His unshakable nearness even in the darkest times.

The more you practice recognizing God in the past, the more quickly you'll come to recognize Him in the present and anticipate His nearness in the future. The more closely you'll feel tied to His heart. The more deeply you'll understand His love.

He *is* with you. He *is* for you. He *is* guiding you. Let's find out how.

Catch the Rain

Here you are invited to open your heart in the presence of Jesus. Please choose *1 or 2 reflection responses* that you are drawn to. You can take time for this. You are worth it.

- Start a gratitude journal, listing at least 10 things each day, big and small, that you experienced as a gift from God.

- Think back over the last 24 hours. When were you most aware of God's presence? Thank Him for how He pursued your attention. When were you the least attuned to God's presence? Confess your distraction and receive His invitation to grow in attunement to Him.

- Consider a particularly challenging or sad experience in your recent past. Ask the Lord to reveal to you how He was at work in and around you during it.

- What correlation do you see between giving thanks and experiencing peace? Consider Psalm 107; Philippians 4:4–9; and 1 Thessalonians 5:12–24.

◖ End each day by thanking God for His constant, active presence in your life. (Refer back to the practice of the *examen* at the start of Part One.)

Face Your Wall

WHATEVER HAS BROUGHT YOU HERE, be it a busy, successful ministry you can't keep up with or a failing, floundering one, be it battles in your personal life or persecution and hardship without, I can promise you this: God can redeem it. That's His business. That's His trademark. That process—turning struggle and pain into redemption and joy—is, in fact, a predictable part of your spiritual journey.

Just as your body matures from infant to toddler to child to adolescent to adult, so your spirit matures, as well. Although it's rarely this linear, often looping backward multiple times, the generally accepted stages of the life of a Christ-follower can be outlined as such:

- Initial trust in Christ, choosing to follow Him
- Being discipled and learning God's Word
- Participating in service or ministry
  - o Encountering a spiritual wall
- Deeper understanding of self and God
- Partnership with the Spirit in serving others
- Living in and out of abiding union with Christ[1]

We hear a lot about the first three stages in our churches, but there is often an acute silence when it comes to the last three and the spiritual wall that you must pass through to get there. However, if you follow Jesus to the point of active ministry, you will undoubtedly encounter a wall at some point.

I'm not a marathon runner, but I have friends who are, and I've heard about the dreaded "runner's wall." It's the point where your body is depleted of stored energy, and it feels as if you've run your race straight into the side of a building. Carrying on without any replenishment is not only incredibly hard, but it can also lead to physical effects akin to inebriation, or even to hospitalization.[2]

All the training in the world cannot prevent the wall. At some point, it's inevitable. Because they know the wall is coming, long-distance runners can prepare for it. We can do the same in our spiritual journey.

Understood correctly, a spiritual wall is a beautiful opportunity. It is a point of transition in the life of a believer. In fact, it might be more aptly described as a locked door than a wall. There is a key to open it, but you have to know where to look.

In their book, *Journey of the Soul: A Practical Guide to Emotional and Spiritual Growth*, Bill and Kristi Gaultiere say that the wall is "a transition season, not a stage. Either we deny our distress and stay busy [in service] or we process our pain and questions to develop a deeper and more authentic faith."[3]

There's the key: realizing that we're in a place of pain and choosing to dive headlong into it with God. The alternative choice of persevering in busyness and dry spiritual disciplines at best may lead to complete burnout, at worst a moral collapse.

Struggling through the repeating cycle of hitting a wall of spiritual fatigue, renewing your determination to serve God better, finding an emptiness in your service again, then redoubling or reworking your ministry efforts is what might be called a time of wandering in the wilderness. You keep falling backward in the stages in an attempt to hurdle the wall, but each time you face it, it only appears higher.

Your efforts alone, no matter how well-intentioned, will not get you past the wall.

We moved to Thailand from Alaska in 2014 on a wing, a prayer, and a dime. Almost literally. But, regardless, we knew we were called to use teaching as missions, and we'd found a new opportunity to do it. We couldn't welcome the change soon enough.

In the two-month transition we had between the end of one school year and the start of the next on the other side of the world, Troy and I had some this-needs-to-change conversations.

"I think we should wait a year before taking on any extracurricular activities, don't you?" I asked (okay, begged). He agreed.

Then he ended up coaching basketball and advising the student council.

"Let's be better at keeping up a weekly date night," he encouraged. I agreed.

We managed something closer to a monthly date night.

"We can just buy a program and self-study Thai," I exclaimed. He agreed.

Seven years later, neither of us are close to fluent yet.

The best-laid plans are good, and the best-kept boundaries better, but even those will not fuel our ministry or prevent the wall.

The Gaultieres suggest that the work at the wall is to simply rest. Wait. Seek empathy. And rest some more. Your experience here might be akin to the "battle" at Jericho, where no fighting ever took place because the Lord acted on behalf of His people. Here at the wall, you are on the cusp of breaking through into new spiritual territory. A settled position in God's land of abundant life awaits. But a sword won't get you there. Your wall can only be broken with a quiet humility and a heart of worship, even when you don't yet see a reason to praise.

If you find your arms heavy and your heart aching as you face your wall, know this: you are on holy ground. The Lord is here, even in this darkness of your soul, and there is victory yet to come. Only be still.[4]

Now when Joshua was near Jericho, he looked up and saw a man standing in front of him with a drawn sword in his hand. Joshua went up to him and asked, "Are you for us or for our enemies?"

"Neither," he replied, "but as commander of the army of the Lord I have now come." Then Joshua fell facedown to the ground in reverence, and asked him, "What message does my Lord have for his servant?"

The commander of the Lord's army replied, "Take off your sandals, for the place where you are standing is holy." And Joshua did so. (Joshua 5:13–15)

Catch the Rain

Here you are invited to open your heart in the presence of Jesus. Please choose *1 or 2 reflection responses* that you are drawn to. You can take time for this. You are worth it.

- Draw a basic timeline of the major events and transitions in your life. Next, attempt to identify where you passed into the first three stages of maturity (Trusting Christ, Discipleship, Service). Is there a point, or several points, where you can identify a wall?

- Hitting the wall can be attributed to internal factors, such as overworking, lack of boundaries, and unresolved sin. It can also be triggered by external factors such as a family crisis, church conflict, or false teaching. Do you recognize any of these influences in your life?

- Meditate on Joshua 5:13–6:21. Imagine yourself in the story. What does God highlight to you?

- List all the "good" things you are doing. Ask the Lord to reveal which of these you're attempting to handle in your own strength.

42

List all the spiritual disciplines you participate in (both private and corporate). Which ones feel dry right now? It's okay to lay those aside for a season or change how you're doing them. Which ones stir your joy and love? Lean into those.

Common Spiritual Disciplines:

Fasting
Prayer
Study
Simplicity
Solitude
Service
Confession
Worship
Meditation
Celebration

Part 2
THE SHADOW OF HIS WINGS

The soul is like a wild animal—tough, resilient, savvy, self-sufficient and yet exceedingly shy. If we want to see a wild animal, the last thing we should do is to go crashing through the woods, shouting for the creature to come out. But if we are willing to walk quietly into the woods and sit silently for an hour or two at the base of a tree, the creature we are waiting for may well emerge, and out of the corner of an eye we will catch a glimpse of the precious wildness we seek.

— Parker Palmer, *A Hidden Wholeness: The Journey Toward an Undivided Life* [1]

CATCH THE RAIN

KEY STEP:
CREATE SAFETY

In Part Two, I'll share about the need for safe spaces to facilitate healing. One helpful practice to guide you through this section is the Sabbath.

The weekly practice of Sabbath was first given to us by God as He modeled it right after Creation. He restated it in the Ten Commandments, and He lived it—albeit with an edginess that defied legalism—through the life of Jesus. Here are some important reminders about the Sabbath:

- It is a gift given for our good
- It's a radical expression of trust in God, not self
- Be prepared to fight for it; the Western World and the prince of this world do not like holy rest
- It takes time to find a weekly rhythm of rest on the Sabbath—make adaptations and keep trying
- To practically facilitate Sabbath keeping, try turning off your phone for the day, starting with a special meal, lighting a candle, and gathering with community for worship and enjoyment of the Lord

The Gift of Rest

I WALKED SLOWLY DOWN THE hill toward my parents' house. My daughter scooted ahead of me on her sled as I gripped the tether so she wouldn't catapult off the driveway and into the woods. This was her first time sledding, after all. The trees stood in frozen silence around us; the sky hung low like a canopy over a down bed. My boots crunched snow. My daughter giggled her delight. But all around us, the stillness stretched her silent arms.

I felt her embrace in a way I usually couldn't in my messy, harried missionary-mom life. The peace was tangible in the serene snowflakes that began to flutter from the sky as we reached the bottom of the hill. We were home for Christmas for the first time in five years, but it wasn't the holly jolly activities that gave it such meaning. It was moments like this one right here. Still. Quiet. Peaceful. And so expansive that I could take a deeper breath than I had in a long time.

That moment was a gift. That moment was a Sabbath.

I've discovered in recent years that those moments of deep inhalation and even deeper exhale can come at any time and in almost any place if I am wide awake to the Spirit's presence in my life. However, it's easy for me to get carried away with plans, activities, and the voices around me to the degree that I find myself holding my breath for much, much longer than is healthy. Our Father knows we're prone to this. And He has woven a rhythm into the pattern of our weeks and lives that offers us this breathing room—if we will accept it.

As we set out in this section of the book to discover and establish safe spaces, the Sabbath offers us a key place to begin. Simply put, we need safety to heal. More than likely, the pressures and disappointments of a life of service and ministry have left their mark on your heart. If you sat with God during any of the reflection responses from the last section, you're beginning to acknowledge the wounds, and, I hope, you're beginning to see the nearness of the Healer in a new way, too. Now, we will begin to establish boundaries and practices that provide the setting for Abba to tend to your soul.

One of the primary shifts that can bring our hearts closer to healing and our lives closer to fullness is to stop viewing God's Word as a command and start viewing it as an invitation. From the beginning, the Creator has extended His hand to man and offered to walk with him. He has established rules to teach us how to live rightly before Him and with others, but He allows us to choose our own way. He has, indeed, made the consequences of our choice apparent, but, ever the patient Father, He allows His prodigal children to leave when they wish.

This—our free will—is a gift of His love. Our choice to return that love is a gift back to Him.

Right in the middle of this loving relationship are invitations to live abundant and full lives as His children. His best is extended to us. When He says, "Go into all the world and make disciples[1]," He is also saying "You're invited to partner with me in bringing my glorious kingdom to earth!" And when He says, "Remember the Sabbath and keep it holy[2]," He is also saying "I'm giving you the gift of a day to enter my rest. Will you join me?"

I haven't always received His commands as invitations. I've seen them as have-tos and or-elses. I've felt their weight as a burden and obliged myself to carry them like a good soldier. However, with the demands of motherhood and the expectations of ministry supporters and school life, it all became too much to bear. Some days I wanted to buck it off and run free.

But then I awoke to grace and a deeper realization that God wasn't placing these burdens on my shoulders; He was offering to carry them with me, giving me the lighter side of the yoke. This verse, though painfully overused, never ceases to speak to me:

Are you tired? Worn out? Burned out on religion? Come to me. Get away with me and you'll recover your life. I'll show you how to take a real rest. Walk with me and work with me—watch how I do it. Learn the unforced rhythms of grace. I

49

*won't lay anything heavy or ill-fitting on you.
Keep company with me and you'll learn to live
freely and lightly.* (Matthew 11:28–30 MSG)

Jesus will give me rest. Jesus will give *you* rest. His
invitation is rest. His cure for the weary life is Sabbath.
And it has been for millennia.

At the bottom of that snowy hill on that still winter
day, I discovered the gift of Sabbath is only unwrapped by
a fully present heart. Later that afternoon, curled up by the
fireplace, I attempted to hold on to the wonder of that
moment by writing these words:

*Snowflakes dance from the sky like down filling from an
angel pillow-fight.
They lilt along merrily, casually, no particular
destination, just enjoying the journey from sky to terra
firma.
Some descend solo, some in a lacy crochet.
I stick out my tongue, eager to melt one, to consume its
icy fluff.
But they're evasive in their swirling dance.
Then I remember my daughter—the girl raised in the
tropics—and I extend to her the first snowflake catching
challenge she has ever received.
Her eyes twinkle as she accepts, opening her mouth with a
puff of visible air.*

We walk slowly on, she and I, with our tongues steaming
and pink against the white backdrop of road and trees
and sky.
"They're hard to catch," she says. I nod.
But like bubbles released from a wand and blown by the
wind, the joy is in the chase; for the instant you catch one,
it's gone.
So I slow time to pace with the lazy dance of the
cascading crystals.
And, in that moment, I catch the peace of God.

Do you have any markers that help you slow the pace of time and catch the peace of God? I won't elaborate on the full meaning of Sabbath here—there are others who have done that with remarkable clarity already[3]—but I do want to remind you of God's invitation to open His gift of rest.

"If you keep your feet from breaking the Sabbath
and from doing as you please on my holy day,
if you call the Sabbath a delight
and the LORD's holy day honorable,
and if you honor it by not going your own way
and not doing as you please or speaking idle
words,
then you will find your joy in the LORD,
and I will cause you to ride in triumph on the
heights of the land
and to feast on the inheritance of your father
Jacob."
  The mouth of the LORD has spoken. (Isaiah 58:13–14)

51

Catch the Rain

Here you are invited to open your heart in the presence of Jesus. Please choose *1 or 2 reflection responses* that you are drawn to. You can take time for this. You are worth it.

- What is your regular practice of Sabbath? If it's not consistent now, when was it (if ever) regularly celebrated in your life? Reflect on your Sabbath experience. Dream of what you want it to be like.

- Special occasions are often marked by specific rituals. What can you do as a weekly remembrance at the beginning of your Sabbath time? Consider a unique candle, song, or food.

- Psalm 92 is noted as a song for the Sabbath. Read it slowly three times. Ask the Holy Spirit to highlight significant words or phrases to you, and write those down to meditate on further.

- List your frequent obstacles to practicing Sabbath. Make a plan for how to eliminate one or two of those obstacles.

The Sanctuary of Home

THE TINY, HOMEMADE SANDBOX WAS a hot commodity in our neighborhood. As was the archway climber a friend had gifted to us and the blow-up kiddie pool we'd purchased. Perfect for my three-year old son and our neighbor's children, we'd spend hours playing in our small yard—much to the amusement of the deaf, old man across the street, our landlord who lived next to him, and the single dad who lived just over the fence to our left.

Many hot afternoons, Lueng (Thai for "uncle"), would hobble across the road to our gate, let himself in, and attempt to communicate with me while we watched the children play. He had never been taught sign language, so in a beautifully simple way it made no difference to him what language I spoke. He used his grunts and gestures the same way to communicate with everyone. His method of neighborhood gossip was quite entertaining and soon I felt surprisingly privy to the problems of neighbors that his hand motions told.

He watched what happened around him—his entire world consisting of one street—and took it upon himself to be the neighborhood reporter. Which also meant he observed and told tales of us, the curious, new foreign family. While I recognized Lueng's innocence behind this, it didn't lessen the stress of feeling like we lived in a fishbowl. For some, this might not matter, but for me, a girl raised in the woods without any neighbors for miles, it grew to be an exhausting strain.

As much as I enjoyed our neighborhood and grew to love Lueng, when a newer house that bordered an empty lot opened up a couple of blocks away, I jumped at the chance to rent it. We ignored Lueng's warnings about the ferocious dog that would now live across from us, shrugged our shoulders about having neighbors immediately out our back door, and carted our belongings down the street to settle into our new home that had six-foot tall windows on two sides of the living and dining room.

Still, it felt like a giant leap in the direction of feeling secure and at peace in our own home. And, for the most part, it was. Then a boy, a couple of years older than my son, showed up at our gate one day. He saw my kids playing in the yard and wanted to join. I warmly invited him in.

We soon discovered that Gee was a bit rough around the edges. The only English words he knew were curse words, he'd attempt to hide our toys in his pockets (one time even in his mouth) before he left, and he consistently disregarded our request that he not play in our yard if we weren't home. Eventually, we scrapped together pieces of his story and learned that his parents weren't in the picture, and he was cared for by his grandparents, who sold

54

pomelo (similar to a grapefruit) at the entrance to our neighborhood.

I tried for months to extend the love of Christ to this boy. I knew his home life was difficult and I wanted to be a refuge for him, but the language barrier consistently left me frustrated and him uncertain. My children began to resent his appearance and would beg me to tell him to go home, but I forced the issue, asking them to be hospitable even when it was uncomfortable.

One day, we returned from an outing to find our gate left open, the hose running, mud all over our front porch, and handprints smeared across the sliding doors where the rocky mud had scratched the glass. I had had enough. *I'm sorry*, I told Jesus, *but I just can't do this anymore.* And the next time Gee came over, I told him he could no longer play at our house.

My children were visibly relieved, while I felt a sickening sense of failure.

If you haven't picked up on it already, I struggle with saying no. I like to help, to be sought out, to be—if I'm honest—given value by what I can contribute. During this season of coming to the end of my hospitality toward Gee, I began to discover the gift of *no* in other areas, too. Because *no* to something I'm not meant to take on is a better *yes* to what I am.

We've since moved into yet another house in a smaller neighborhood closer to the rice fields. I can see more stars out here. I can watch the fireflies from the back porch. We can own cats without the neighborhood street cats trying to impregnate them or claw their eyes out each night. And, most importantly, I feel more at rest and secure in my own home. That, in turn, allows me to give more to the areas I *am* sure God is calling me to: mothering, writing, women's ministry, helping at our international school.

Do I still feel guilty about all this? About moving away from curious Lueng? About refusing to let Gee play at our house? About the many other times I've said no in the past few years? Sometimes, yes. But mostly, no. Because those particular places of extending myself were not even done for Jesus so much as they were done for myself with the wrong motives. And continuing to put myself and my family in a place that wore us thin by its mere proximity to certain things and people was not something God was asking me to do.

Could he be asking you to forsake a comfortable home and live in the slums? Travel the road preaching? Dwell in the inner city to reach those you're called to minister to? Absolutely.

But could it also be that you're allowing your home, your privacy, your family time, or your things to be run over and muddied time and again simply because you haven't discerned what *no* God might be allowing you to say to make room for a better *yes*? That's for you to decide.

Either way, it's an invitation. An invitation to a *yes* somewhere. And it will take much Holy Spirit guidance to figure out. But, please hear this: *healing and restoration happen best in places of safety.*

If you find yourself barely hanging on to the relationships that should matter most, give them whatever space is needed to mend. And if you're not sure if you can continue to pour yourself out to those around you much longer, please don't push yourself all the way to burnout. Pause to determine where and how you can create a physical sanctuary.

Your home is a good place to start. Even if that means moving a few houses down the street.

Catch the Rain

Here you are invited to open your heart in the presence of Jesus. Please choose *1 or 2 reflection responses* that you are drawn to. You can take time for this. You are worth it.

- What words would you use to describe your home right now? List as many as you can, then evaluate them to see if they speak of safety and rest, or not.

- Spend time in Psalm 23. What is the Good Shepherd's heart for you?

- For a week, keep track of the people and events in your home. Are they life-giving or draining to you? Are they God's *yes* for you in this season?

- Journal about the last time you said *no* to something—particularly something that was good or that you cared about. What was the result of that *no* in your life?

Lines in Pleasant Places

A CHANGE WAS COMING, AND as I stared at it from every possible angle, I could only see one outcome: I would go back into teaching. It just made sense. My youngest was about to enter kindergarten at the international school in Thailand where we came to serve. My degree was in elementary education. The need, as always, was for more volunteer teachers. How could I not?

Only, I didn't really want to teach. My last experience teaching kindergarten through fifth grade in a single classroom in remote Alaska was challenging, to put it mildly. The more I thought about it, the more I recognized that teaching, while I enjoyed it, was exhausting for me. And so was mothering. I wasn't sure I could handle both at the same time—at least not with much grace.

At that time, I was in a book study group, and the author[1] prompted us to take serious stock of our lives—our commitments, our experiences, our hopes and even our childhood dreams. I almost didn't allow myself to go down that road. I knew it would lead to places of disappointment and that nagging sense of duty I always lived with. But walk it I did, and what I discovered surprised me.

I was made to be a writer.

I'll share more about that later in this book, but, for now, my point is this: I had been ignoring both my desires and my design because I was allowing my sense of responsibility to dictate my choices. *All that money for college, I should use my degree. So much need within the community, I should fill in the holes. Such a powerful opportunity to touch lives, I should take it.*

But what I began to discover in that season, is that I can only offer my true self to God. Nothing else is worthy. Not who I wish I was. Not who I think He wants me to be. Not who others push me to be. Not who makes the most sense for this situation. Just me.

And *just me* needs more quiet space than noise. I come alive when I create something meaningful with words. Writing, for me, is a form of listening prayer that connects me to my Father's heart like little else. If I do not draw protective lines around the time and space I need for quiet and for words, I stagnate. Shrivel, even. And I cease to offer my truest, deepest worship to God.

There's an interconnectivity between this, my lines and my worship. My life and my offering. And, naturally, the way God can use me to touch the world. I believe this is a truth that encompasses you, too. *A life lived within the bounds of who God made you to be is an act of submission to your Creator that He can use to bring His kingdom according to His design.*

Again, I remember, this is all much less about me than I like to think it is. It's not about you, either. At least, not in the self-important way we often slide into in our ministry and service roles.

We serve a boundless God with unlimited resources. He does not need us to accomplish His will. But, He wants us to partner with Him by joyfully living out of our unique design. *That's* where we give Him the best, the first fruits, of our service.

> *Lord, you alone are my portion and my cup;*
> *   you make my lot secure.*
> *The boundary lines have fallen for me in pleasant*
> *places;*
> *   surely I have a delightful inheritance.*
> *I will praise the Lord, who counsels me;*
> *   even at night my heart instructs me.*
> *I keep my eyes always on the Lord.*
> *   With him at my right hand, I will not be shaken.*
> (Psalm 16:5–8)

David seems to grasp it here. The Lord is enough. And I, in Him, am enough. "The boundary lines have fallen for me in pleasant places. . ." He not only accepts what he has been given, he delights in it. "Surely I have a delightful inheritance."

Is what you have been given enough? Is who you are enough?

Go ahead and sit with those questions for a moment.

Many of us have been trained to ask the question, is what I *do* enough? But let me have the privilege to tell you that you are not loved or valued because you got the job done. Are you hearing that? (Somebody please remind me of this tomorrow because it's such a hard truth for me to hold onto!) Your belovedness and worth are firmly established in Christ. Unshakably and for eternity, He is delighted in you. In fact, He sings over you.[2]

You have nothing to prove, only the joyful opportunity to be who God made you to be and to discover what He designed you to do. As you learn and grow and the world around you changes, the roles you take will change, too. That's okay. As we love to watch our children discover and develop their talents and interests, so, too, God must cheer for us as we try, fail, learn, and try again.

As you grapple with these questions and consider your own boundary lines, I want to offer one other consideration: it *is* okay to ask the Lord for more. Not from a heart of discontent or striving or power-seeking, but from a place of humility that cries out "I need more of you, Jesus! Live out your love and peace and justice and grace through me in ways I could never imagine. Increase my capacity to know you, and in knowing you to become like you."

Here's my case in point: I'm back in the classroom. Now, after several years, many prayers, and much growth, I'm teaching again. Not out of duty or obligation, but out of joy. I am delighting in a new season of meaningful work, and yet I still sit here tending these words. The Lord has expanded my boundary lines, and I will praise Him all the more.

If you feel that you've lost your true self to your work or ministry, here is your invitation to return to your wide-eyed, eighteen-year-old self and see the realm of possibilities before you.

Who are you? What are your deepest desires? What adventure is God inviting you to take with Him? Just as life felt scary and uncertain at eighteen, these questions might shake you up a bit now. I know. They did for me, too. But you wouldn't be reading this book now if I hadn't asked them.

Catch the Rain

Here you are invited to open your heart in the presence of Jesus. Please choose *1 or 2 reflection responses* that you are drawn to. You can take time for this. You are worth it.

- Ask the Lord to help you answer the questions posed in this chapter: Who are you? What are your deepest desires? What adventure is God inviting you to take with Him?

- Have a parent or long-time friend sit with you and help you remember your childhood dreams and the things that used to make you come alive.

- List all the roles you do, the "hats" you wear. Which ones fit well? Which ones are the most ill-fitting? What will you do about it?

- Get out a calendar and create specific boundaries to guard the time and space you need to do something that makes you feel like *you*. (Hint: This will be something you love. Is it hiking? Music? Reading? Baking? Sports? Organizing? Painting? Gardening? Coffee with a friend?)

Out of Hiding

THE WOMEN IN THE CONFERENCE room sat silently, the atmosphere heavy with emotion after three brave ladies shared their testimonies. They carried stories of incredible loss and grace, silent struggles and healing, broken relationships and redemption. Every woman in that room could relate on some level.

Yet, as usual after testimonies of tragedy turned to triumph, I felt almost annoyingly sheltered. I didn't bear the badge of losing a close loved one, battling chronic illness, or contending for wayward children. So why did I feel so weighed down and weary? I had it easy.

Then, almost as an afterthought, one of the ladies added this: "The little pains count, too. Don't ignore them because they can add up like one hundred tiny paper cuts." *Ouch*.

I wrestled with this idea—the validity of each little struggle and disappointment—through the entire morning. By the afternoon, however, I decided to give it a go. I found an outdoor table, opened my journal, and poised my pen to list out every pain and sorrow I could think of from the past year. I was about to crack open the can of an outwardly blessed but inwardly tumultuous season of my life in young motherhood and missions.

It felt wrong.

Counting my blessings, yes. Counting my pains? I don't know, Lord.

But the seal on that can had already been broken and the memories began leaking out unbidden. So, I wrote. And wrote and wrote and wrote.

As I asked God to help me name the pains, these words surfaced: lonely, silenced, helpless, scared, trapped, jealous, hopeless. Real words. Real pains. And I began to see how one hundred untended paper cuts had scarred and calloused my heart. I saw the armor I had built in a pathetic attempt to shield myself from more pain. For the first time in a long time, I really saw myself.

"Ignoring our emotions is turning our back on reality. Listening to our emotions ushers us into reality. And reality is where we meet God... Emotions are the language of the soul. They are the cry that gives the heart a voice," writes Peter Scazzero.[1] To ignore our heart cries, our pains, and the situations that cause them is a path that leads not to strength but to hardness of heart, not to joy but to a soul-numbing stagnation.

Joy and pain are joined at the hip. You can't ignore one without rejecting the other. Both are tools that God uses to awaken us and turn our hearts toward Him. But a heart calloused and shut down to pain is similarly walled off to the full vibrancy of joy.

The theme of that year's regional women's retreat was "Deep." It evoked imagery of the unending depths of God's love, but also the unsearchable depths of man's (in this case, woman's) heart, and the meeting of the two where God's grace is most fully known on troubled waters.

My soul thirsts for God, for the living God.
   When can I go and meet with God?
My tears have been my food
   day and night,
while people say to me all day long,
   "Where is your God?"
These things I remember
   as I pour out my soul:
how I used to go to the house of God
   under the protection of the Mighty One
with shouts of joy and praise
   among the festive throng. . .

My soul is downcast within me;
   therefore I will remember you. . .
Deep calls to deep
   in the roar of your waterfalls;
all your waves and breakers
   have swept over me. (Psalm 42:2–4, 6a, 7)

This Psalm of the sons of Korah is a brave venture into pain. It depicts longing, sorrow, verbal assault from others, nostalgia, and uncertainty if God would rescue or allow the writer to drown in the middle of the trial.

And yet. . .

> *By day the Lord directs his love,*
> *at night his song is with me—*
> *a prayer to the God of my life.*
>
> *I say to God my Rock,*
> *"Why have you forgotten me?*
> *Why must I go about mourning,*
> *oppressed by the enemy?". . .*
>
> *Why, my soul, are you downcast?*
> *Why so disturbed within me?*
> *Put your hope in God,*
> *for I will yet praise him,*
> *my Savior and my God.* (Psalm 42:8–9, 11)

This "prayer to the God of my life" is an intermingling of sorrow and comfort, doubt and trust, pain and praise. It plumbs the depths of both. So, too, can your conversations with the Lord.

When poured out to Jesus, your colicky baby and those sleepless nights, the bickering and disunity with your spouse, the rejection from not being invited to that gathering, the disappointment from your idea being voted down, the flat tires and ant infestations and unanswered emails—need I go on? Every bit of that becomes grounds for redemption when exposed and surrendered to the One whose business is to make all things new.

This is all summed up beautifully by Brennan Manning: "If we conceal our wounds out of fear and shame, our inner darkness can neither be illuminated nor become a light for others."[2]

There is both healing for you and hope for others in the raw flesh of your pain.

After that retreat, I went home and, with much trepidation, shared my list of paper-cut scars with Troy. He listened. He received it without offense. He confessed where he, too, had felt hurt and had retreated emotionally to be "safe." And, miracle of miracles, we began to experience renewed joy. Many of those pains I'd listed—feeling silenced, lonely, and hopeless—dissipated, and the journey toward healing began.

I may not have a dramatic story of surviving abuse, burying a child, or battling depression, but I do have a testimony, and it is this: the enemy tried to deceive me into believing that brushing aside my frustrations and struggles would make me more mature and productive, but my Savior revealed His tenderness toward my every pain, caught all my tears, and turned those tears into raindrops to heal my soul.

CATCH THE RAIN

Even in our pain, we can catch the rain.

Catch the Rain

Here you are invited to open your heart in the presence of Jesus. Please choose *1 or 2 reflection responses* that you are drawn to. You can take time for this. You are worth it.

- What is your internal reaction to the idea of naming your pain? Do you have resistance to it? Ask the Lord to help you understand why.

- Sit with Psalm 42 and meditate on the verses that stir something within you (good, hard, or otherwise). Some other psalms for this include 69, 40, and 86.

- If you are ready, ask Jesus to sit with you and help you name your pain. Start with the past week (you can go back further as needed) and ask: What made me sad or angry? What disappointed me? What words have I held back?

- If you've named your pain, you've let Jesus illuminate it. Now that it's standing before you, ask the Lord to help you see it with His eyes. What does He reveal to you about these experiences and your feelings?

I Hear You, Friend

FRIENDSHIP. DOES THAT WORD EVOKE feelings of warmth or sadness in you? Perhaps a bit of both. In some seasons, friendship comes easily. Falls into our lap. Yet other seasons seem bereft of the deep connection and joy of friendship. I can't offer a remedy for this—life is undeniably full of relational ups and downs—but I can suggest a framework for an intentional kind of spiritual friendship that releases healing and hope into your life through one essential facet: empathetic listening.

"Empathy is a strange and powerful thing. There is no script. There is no right way or wrong way to do it. It's simply listening, holding space, withholding judgment, emotionally connecting, and communicating that incredibly healing message of 'You're not alone.' "[1]

I am, quite frankly, still learning how to do this, how to *be* this kind of listener, but I've had a few great examples to learn from.

Our family doctor in the States is a busy father with an ever-growing practice. His life and schedule are overflowing with demands, and yet, when we sit in his office, we're welcomed with a genuine smile and a few sincere questions about life in general before he asks what we're concerned about physically. As we share, he listens and nods, maybe takes a note or two, and then (here's the key), he asks follow-up questions. He doesn't jump to a conclusion, slap a prescription in our palm, and scoot us out the door. He is genuinely interested in our well-being and will keep asking questions until there are no more. *Then*, when we've come to a satisfactory conclusion for that issue, he inevitably asks if we have any other concerns. In all this, he makes us feel as if we are his only patients for the entire day. He does this for every single person. Now that's a good listener and an excellent doctor.

Then there's my friend, Julie, who takes empathetic listening to another level entirely. She's what I might call a "soul doctor," although I imagine she'd laugh off that title. When Julie asks me how I am, she stops whatever she is doing, looks deep into my eyes, often grabs my arm, and waits. I know she's not hoping I'll say "Fine!" so she can get back to business. She wants to hear my heart, and, as I share, she nods her understanding and reflects my emotions in her own expression. She has this incredible (also sometimes annoying) way of releasing my pent-up tears. And often with only her presence and a gentle touch.

These are rare people, aren't they? The friends who will sit with you and not try to solve your problems, the ones who ask questions more than give platitudes or interrupt with their own stories—these are the people who we feel safe with. These are the healers.

If we are to continue on this path of soul restoration, we're going to need some friends to journey it with us. We need to feel the comfort of Abba through the love of others. Unfortunately, empathetic listening doesn't seem to come naturally to many people. However, with a bit of guidance and practice, this skill *can* be developed. As suggested by Brian K. Rice, an intentional, spiritual friendship can be chosen by two people who are like-minded, committed, encouraging, discerning, comforting, focused on the work of Christ, and willing to confess their sins to one another and pray for each other.[2] Both friends need to desire this depth of authentic connection and be willing to invest time into their relationship.

This spiritual friendship can have as many ways to connect as desired, but, at its core, it needs a time (usually weekly) set aside for intentionally sharing about what God is doing in your life. Not the external situations that are a struggle or a joy, but the internal work of the Spirit in the middle of those situations. One friend shares while the other one listens. Really, prayerfully listens.

In response to this sharing, Bible verses aren't stamped over troubles and advice isn't given; instead, questions are asked. Questions like, How are you experiencing Jesus in this? What are you feeling about that? How do you sense Jesus responding to that feeling? Why do you think God is moving in your life in this way right now? What response do you sense God leading you to?

Then the tables turn. The other friend shares about what is going on in their spiritual life, their heart of hearts, while the other simply listens and responds with questions. This can also be done in a group of three or four if enough time is allowed.

It sounds contrived. Forced. I know, but once this pattern for soul-level conversation is established it becomes sacred ground for deepening your relationship with Christ and furthering your healing. I am incredibly thankful for and indebted to the precious friends who have walked with me in this capacity—both formally and informally—over the years. I've seen Jesus through you, dear ones.

To begin, consider this tried-and-true adage: be the kind of friend you wish you had. The wisdom in that is a good place to start—turn your ear and heart toward those around you more often, and you just might find them returning empathetic listening to you. Perhaps out of those conversations, God will naturally reveal a like-minded soul thirsting after Christ, and, with a little nurturing, you can grow in spiritual friendship together.

Author and speaker, Jennie Allen highlights the intentionality and vulnerability of all this when she says, "Here's the thing: you're gonna be as close as you are vulnerable enough to share. You have to be the one that goes first. . . I'm a big believer in not giving up on people too fast. I think most people want to go deep. We can't just be looking for the person that is poised and as deep as you are. Sometimes you need to help them get there and that's a worthwhile pursuit. I believe most people want to go there and they just don't know how. We get to be the people that are there for them, pull it out of them, and let them be vulnerable."[3]

It might be scary or awkward. You might even flop a time or two as you're reaching out to people, but it's worth it in the end. If you're in the never-ending plains of flighty friendships, let me empower you with this: *you can facilitate the setting and relationships for the kind of empathetic listening your soul craves.* You don't have to have a pastor or a counselor (although those are good, too!); you simply need a friend.

Catch the Rain

Here you are invited to open your heart in the presence of Jesus. Please choose *1 or 2 reflection responses* that you are drawn to. You can take time for this. You are worth it.

- Reflect on a time that empathetic listening has been offered to you. How did it help you?

- Do you have a spiritual friend or two already? If so, do you have a regular time to meet with them? If it's infrequent, can you make space for a weekly meeting?

- List 3–6 people you would enjoy spiritual friendship with. (Remember, they should be like-minded, committed, encouraging, discerning, comforting, focused on the work of Christ, and willing to confess their sins and pray for you.) Prayerfully choose one to suggest this idea to.

- Meditate on biblical examples when Jesus was an empathetic listener or asked meaningful questions. (You might start with Matt. 20:20–34)

Part 3
THE SHAPE OF YOUR SOUL

*When Jesus came to the region of Caesarea Philippi,
he asked his disciples, "Who do people say the Son of
Man is?"*

*They replied, "Some say John the Baptist; others say
Elijah; and still others, Jeremiah or one of the
prophets."*

*"But what about you?" he asked. "Who do you say I
am?"*

*Simon Peter answered, "You are the Messiah, the Son
of the living God."*

*Jesus replied, "Blessed are you, Simon son of Jonah,
for this was not revealed to you by flesh and blood, but
by my Father in heaven. And I tell you that you are
Peter, and on this rock I will build my church, and the
gates of Hades will not overcome it.*

— Matthew 16:13–18

KEY STEP:
GET PERSONAL

In Part Three, we're getting personal. I'll offer some ideas for how to get to know yourself and Jesus, and how the two of you connect best. One significant practice to guide you through this section is understanding the *spiritual pathways.*

Don't be misled by the phrasing of spiritual pathways. It doesn't indicate multiple routes to Heaven. Jesus is the only way. Period. But spiritual pathways does indicate that we each have a unique design and there will be unique ways that are most natural and joyful for us to connect with God. The last chapter in this section dives into that specifically, but for now, start by asking yourself these questions:

- Where do I notice God's presence most easily?
- When is my heart drawn to worship?
- Do I find it easier to pray alone or with a group?
- Do I have a lot of physical reminders of God's love in my home? Or do I prefer simplicity?
- Am I fired up or fearful when presented with an opportunity to help bring justice?
- What kind of church service do I enjoy most?
- What kind of books feed my soul?

Seek My Face

I COULDN'T STAND UP ANYMORE. I'd been sick for a week, but this was the big annual conference—the event I'd been praying for, preparing for, and coordinating for months. I was there, but I had nothing left to give. I slumped into a heap on the floor as the weight of the songs of worship pressed in around me. Clinging to my knees, head bowed, I let the tears come. Tears I so often held back out of my desire to appear strong, put-together. Yet here I was—the missionary, the teacher, the mom—at the end of myself, but at the beginning of knowing God in an intimate way I had never experienced before.

That morning, while getting dressed, I had prayed, "God, show me your glory!" I wanted His fullness. I craved His presence. I knew this conference was nothing without Him. What more noble prayer could there be than the prayer of Moses in Exodus 33?

Yet, no sooner had those words left my heart than I heard His gentle reply, "No. I want you to seek my face."

I paused, pants half-zipped. Was that the Lord? And what in the world was the difference between asking for His glory and seeking His face? *Um, okay. Show me your face, then.* I shrugged and zipped my jeans.

That evening, as I puddled on the floor in the front row of the meeting hall, the morning's prayer came back to me. "God," I cried, "show me your face! I feel like I don't know what you look like anymore. Who are you?!"

As I rocked myself in time to the music, an image grew in my mind: a little girl, curled up in her Father's arms. She was held, protected, delighted in, and comforted. "I'm your Daddy," came that still, small voice again.

I had never, before that moment, dared to enter the intimacy of a face-to-face encounter with the King of Kings, Lord of Lords, Ruler of All Creation, God. And yet as sure as I knew I was saved by grace, I knew He was giving me permission to look into His eyes and call Him *Daddy*.

That invitation broke me in the best way. You see, I have a soft spot right in the middle of my heart for my earthly Daddy. He's my champion, my warrior, and my friend. He's a far cry from perfect, but I have never once had reason to question his love or his faithfulness in my life. I know he would do anything to protect his daughters—me, my big sister, and his "adopted" daughter in Thailand— and I couldn't, in all honesty, say I knew that to be true of God.

After all, following God had caused me a lot of pain. I still served and obeyed, but my image of God hung heavily on the side of Master, not Daddy. So, the day God invited me to call Him Daddy was also the day He asked me to release my grudge for leading me through a wilderness. It was the day He asked me to trust His heart of fiercely protective love for me like never before.

Yes, Daddy. I trust You, my heart responded.

From that renewed relationship, I could confidently say that I was loved with the strong and tender embrace of a father who spared nothing—absolutely nothing—to make me His child. I was held by the hands that flung the stars into place. I was known by the One who counted every hair on my head and could hear my words before I thought them.[1]

This revelation changed me. I pray differently now. I read the scriptures through a broader lens. I understand frustrations and pain in my life in a new way. And I wonder if God has an aspect of His character that He wants to reveal to you in a deeply personal way?

Who are you God? That is perhaps the greatest question. And the second is like it: *Who am I, God?*

We each have a unique shape, a bucket that God can fill in ways specific to only you. In that realization, we discover that neither God nor our relationship with Him follows the lines someone else has drawn.

God is wholly other, indescribably vast, and beyond our comprehension. His ways are not our ways nor His thoughts our thoughts, yet His desire to reveal Himself to us and be known is real. Jesus shows us this. Yet, even in the ways He healed—one day a touch, another a word, another a glob of mud, and still another a bath—He maintains the mystery.

There is no formula to God. But there is always a hand reaching out for you with a deeper, more personal revelation of His heart.

When you seek His face, what do you see? I invite you to sit with that question for a moment.

Consider what name you use to address God in prayer, what expression you visualize as you imagine Him looking at you, what scripture you hold to as a favorite revelation of His character. Again, what do you discover when you seek His face?

Hear my voice when I call, Lord;
be merciful to me and answer me.
My heart says of you, "Seek his face!"
  Your face, Lord, I will seek. . .
  I remain confident of this:
  I will see the goodness of the Lord
  in the land of the living.
Wait for the Lord;
  be strong and take heart
  and wait for the Lord. (Psalm 27:7–8, 13–14)

Catch the Rain

Here you are invited to open your heart in the presence of Jesus. Please choose *1 or 2 reflection responses* that you are drawn to. You can take time for this. You are worth it.

- Ask: Who are you, God? Now wait. . .

- List as many names of God as you can think of. Ask the Holy Spirit to highlight one that He wants to demonstrate to you personally. Write it down and note the ways you experience God as _____ this week.

- Place yourself in the story of the prodigal son, found in Luke 15:11–32. You may find that you identify more with either the older or the younger son, and as you imagine yourself in the passage, take note of the father. What does he say? How does he look at you? What feelings does he express? What is his invitation to you?

- What grudges (those places you secretly feel God has wronged you or let you down) are you holding against the Father? Talk to Him honestly

about them, then give Him a chance to respond.
What does He say?

Who Am I?

WHO AM I, GOD? I sat on my bed, legs curled under me, twiddling my pen. As I waited, numerous names and labels I've been given over the years streamed through my thoughts. Corella, Cora, Mom, Mrs. Roberts, teacher, writer, homemaker, event coordinator, missionary, leader, independent, INFJ, Enneagram 3, nature lover. Soon, less-desirable labels followed. Highly sensitive, perfectionist, jack of all trades but master of none, suck-up, undesirable, unworthy, alone. . .

I stopped the thought train before it completely derailed. *But who do You say that I am?* I figured if Jesus could ask it of His disciples, then I could ask it back to Him.

A word fluttered into my mind, delicate as a butterfly, foreign as a seashell in the mountains. I smiled in recognition of the Voice.

I looked up the meaning of the name, and, while I won't divulge its entirety on these pages that are too public for something so precious, I will share that it refers to righteousness and has a connection to a beautiful biblical story.

If that's truly how God sees me, I can let every other name be crushed beneath its weight.

87

A few chapters ago, we began to remember who we are. Or, at least, who we believe ourselves to be. And that's important, but even more important is to understand who God says we are.

We carry around a lot of labels and names—the ones given by our parents, our friends, our vocation, our giftings, and our mistakes. But is this who we are? A composite of all these labels? Or does God say something different?

It would seem that when God wants to state a truth over the life of a follower—especially when that truth is yet to be fully expressed—He does so by changing his name. You likely know the change from Abram and Sarai to Abraham and Sarah; from "exalted father" and "princess" to "father and mother of nations".[1] Then there's Jacob the deceiver to Israel the overcomer.[2] A bit less well-known is that God, through Moses, expanded Hoshea's name to Joshua, meaning not just "salvation" but "Yahweh is salvation," before sending Joshua to lead the Israelites into the Promised Land.[3]

In the New Testament, too, there are a few significant name changes noted. Jesus himself changes Simon's name to Cephas, or Peter. He prophesies that while Simon was still very much only "one who heard" of God's steadfast love, he would one day be a "rock" for the early church, living out of this unchanging love.[4] Even the apostles switched Joseph to Barnabas because he was a "son of encouragement." [5] Incredible.

Except for Barnabas, these new names are given before the bearer has in any way earned the title. They are undeserved proclamations of what God would accomplish through these people. And I think that each new-name-bearer needed the regular reminder of God's good intention for his life as he faced years of waiting, numerous battles, and made terrible mistakes.

Do you need a name like that? One that calls forth who God intends you to be regardless of what your past has labeled you?

One name change I want to explore with you is this remarkable proclamation the Lord makes about Solomon:

> *Then David comforted his wife Bathsheba, and he*
> *went to her and made love to her. She gave birth to*
> *a son, and they named him Solo-*
> *mon. The Lord loved him; and because*
> *the Lord loved him, he sent word through Nathan*
> *the prophet to name him Jedidiah.* (2 Samuel
> 12:24–25)

Solomon means "peaceful," and Jedidiah means "loved by God"—both extraordinary in intent. I wonder if David, after all the giants and battles and fleeing and uprising and murder in his life, earnestly desired peace for his son? And, interestingly, most of Solomon's rule as king was marked by peace and prosperity unlike any other time in Israel.

But what astounds me even more is God's outright adoration of this child. He shouldn't have even been born, given that David never should have taken Bathsheba to be his wife. He shouldn't have been king since he was David's tenth-born son. And should he have even been granted such wisdom and wealth considering that God knew he would turn to worship of false gods later in life?

No, Solomon did *not* deserve the name Jedidiah. Nor do I.

Nonetheless, God looks at him and simply declares him loved, just as He does of you and I in Christ.

But this undeserved belovedness isn't all. Jesus is also holding a new name for you in heaven.

Whoever has ears, let them hear what the Spirit says to the churches. To the one who is victorious, I will give some of the hidden manna. I will also give that person a white stone with a new name written on it, known only to the one who receives it. (Revelation 2:17)

I want that stone. Don't you?

For whatever quirky reason, I love nicknames. Or, as they call it in Thailand, the play-name. Which just fits. It's the name you give to someone you play with that is both short and endearing. It usually signifies something in the history of the relationship. It's intimate.

My firstborn son has had an adorable ferocity about him from the moment he emerged into this world. He quickly earned the nickname Tiger from me, or Tigs for short. I'm the only one in the world who calls him this, and I tend to only use it during special moments of togetherness. It's not what I call him when I remind him to do his homework or call him to the table for supper. He's more likely to hear his full first and middle name then. I didn't intentionally choose to reserve it for times of closeness, it's just that it holds such a special place in our relationship that it only seems appropriate then.

The Father saw your adorable ferocity, or your sensitive depth, or your indomitable perseverance, or your exuberant expressiveness, or your creative ingenuity when you were born, and He spoke a name over you. Jedidiah—loved by God—yes. And also. . . (you fill in the blank here.) What prophetic, intimate name does He have for you?

Catch the Rain

Here you are invited to open your heart in the presence of Jesus. Please choose *1 or 2 reflection responses* that you are drawn to. You can take time for this. You are worth it.

- Ask: Who am I, God? Now wait. . .

- List the many names and titles you carry. Ask God to show you which to hold on to and which to lay down. Maybe some no longer fit you or maybe they hold reminders of past hurt. Courageously cross these off your list.

- If God has revealed a prophetic name or a name of endearment to you, do some research on the meaning of that name. What is God proclaiming over your life through it? Is there a Bible verse associated with it?

- Meditate on the biblical examples of name changes. (Genesis 17 and 32; Numbers 13; 2 Samuel 12; Matthew 16; Acts 4) What else does the Holy Spirit reveal to you as significant?

He Wants My Attention

"HE DOES NOT ASK MUCH of us, merely a thought of Him from time to time, a little act of adoration, sometimes to ask for His grace, sometimes to offer Him our sufferings, at other times to thank Him for the graces, past and present, He has bestowed on us, in the midst of our troubles to take solace in Him as often as we can. Lift up your heart to Him during your meals and in company; the least little remembrance will always be the most pleasing to Him. One need not cry out very loudly; He is nearer to us than we think."[1]

Brother Lawrence, an ordinary monk who discovered the joy of God's presence even while washing dishes[2], presents it so purely for us: God delights in our attention. In our rejoicing and our crying, our going and our staying, our work and our play, our frustration and our celebration. He is already there, longing for us to merely glance His direction in every situation.

What, then, does God do to capture your attention? Are there specific ways that are almost like a touch on the chin, redirecting your eyes toward Him?

I understand God's desire for this more keenly now as my oldest child is beginning to find his independence. He's not my clinging baby nor my look-at-me-mom kid anymore. He's finding his own way, even though I'm still often by his side. Yet, when he turns to me with a smile, asks for my help, confides in me with tears, or comes to me for a hug, I absolutely rejoice—inwardly, of course, so that I don't scare him off.

Is that what it's like for our Father? If so, why is it so hard for me to turn my heart toward Him more often?

I remember a time when we had a plane ticket fiasco. I was anxious, frantic even, while I worked furiously to resolve the issue. Internet searches, phone calls, discussions with Troy to problem solve—we did it all until the solution was found. Then, and only then, did I pause to pray.

I turned to my own abilities, man's wisdom, and the worldwide web before I looked to God. As this dawned on me, I felt a deep conviction. Not only because God might have directed our thoughts and steps more clearly, but also because I simply ignored Him. In my inattentiveness to my loving Father, I missed an opportunity to bring Him joy and to bring myself peace. Lose, lose.

Alternatively, we were driving across the country a few years ago when our van broke down. "Oh, Jesus, help," I whispered, glancing at the nothingness of central Montana around us. We were still a good five hours away from home, and the two-year-old and the four-year-old in the back seat likely wouldn't do too well sitting on the side of the freeway in the summer sun while we waited for a tow truck. How far away was the nearest town, anyway?

As often happens in rural America, the cell phone had no reception, so Troy hopped out and looked around. He recalled seeing a home near the road just a quarter mile back or so, and off he jogged. As the kids and I found a bit of shade to plunk down in, I tried not to worry about the fact that most Montanans own guns and dislike trespassers. "Let's pray," I suggested, and they offered trusting pleas for help.

Eventually, Troy returned. The house he found was owned by a nice pastor. The tow truck would be here soon, and the nearest town was just ten minutes away. *Thank you, Jesus!* As we neared the town, the driver glanced at our kids in the rearview mirror and suggested that he drop us off at the city park where there was a playground and even a swimming pool. *Um, yes, please!*

When we arrived, I called my dad, who said he'd hitch up the trailer to come get us, and I thanked God that he was available to offer help. We swam in the pool, ate dinner at a nearby diner, and generally enjoyed the afternoon. I was amazed. Only God could turn a disaster into a blessing.

And I believe He delighted to do so for His thankful children. Win, win.

Now, as I consider the differences in these two scenarios, I recognize that there were many contributing factors to how my heart responded, once ignoring God, the other time calling out to Him readily. However, one obvious factor sticks out: the accessibility of technology. What if my cell phone had worked on the side of the road next to nowhere in Montana? I believe I would have been much more self-reliant and offered far fewer prayers. I certainly wouldn't have given thanks to the same extent for the beautiful ways God took care of us through both the pastor and the tow truck driver.

I'm not anti-technology by any means, but I do think it's worth remembering that it can be one of our greatest distractions. How often do I ask Google for answers before asking God? What do I reach for first in the morning, my phone or my Bible? What do I respond to more quickly, my message notifications or Holy Spirit nudges?

God's presence is by far the greatest gift we have. I don't want to trade it for a pocket idol.

There's a fair bit of chatter these days about being present. And for good reason, too. The diversions of this world seem to be growing exponentially. Perhaps one of the first steps we must take toward being truly present with God's presence is to identify our pet distractions. Like our phones, many things are good and helpful when used with care, but they become distracting at best and dangerous at worst when they begin to demand the best of our attention.

I think of Matthew 6:20–21, where Jesus says, "But store up for yourselves treasures in heaven, where moths and vermin do not destroy, and where thieves do not break in and steal. For where your treasure is, there your heart will be also."

The draw of our hearts, the focus of our minds, and the effort of our strength reveals our treasure. Am I loving God or something else with my heart, mind, and strength?

It appears to be more difficult than we think. In all honesty, I paused after typing "the" in the previous paragraph to answer a text message. Clearly, I'm writing this chapter for myself first and foremost! We need to get serious about guarding our attention and affections, training them on the One who alone is wholly worthy.

This turning of our attention to God, this practicing His presence, begins with storing up. We store up memories of God's faithfulness, prayers answered, moments of peace amid trial, favorite Bible verses, providential conversations, breathtaking sunsets and caring embraces. These moments of noticing God need to be captured and treasured. Forgetfulness, I believe, is one of man's chief problems.

But taking time to remember rarely happens in the crush of our busy days. Occasionally, we need to retreat. Find a place of solitude. Let our hearts get quiet.

The silence might make us squirm at first. After all, we're accustomed to meeting the demands of our schedule and having our attention yanked in multiple directions at once. With a little practice, however, we can find warm comfort in quiet moments; we'll sense God's presence more readily. Again, this is due to the simple fact that we've actively removed distractions.

In all of this, I find that there is an interwoven growth that occurs. The more we notice His presence, the more willing we are to offer Him ours. The more we think of Him, the more we love Him. The more we love Him, the more we think of Him. Out of the life lived with God flows the ability to be undistracted in the presence of others. Even the key to being present to yourself, unafraid of what you'll find there, is found in learning to first be alive in God's ever-presence.

There are specific ways that God gets your attention and makes you notice His presence. When are those times? What are those moments?

Each one is a raindrop offered to fill your bucket.

"The King, full of mercy and goodness, very far from chastising me, embraces me with love, makes me eat at His table, serves me with His own hands, gives me the key of His treasures; He converses and delights Himself with me incessantly, in a thousand ways, and treats me in all respects as His favorite. It is thus I consider myself from time to time in His holy presence."[3]

May you find yourself from time to time at His table, in His holy presence today.

Catch the Rain

Here you are invited to open your heart in the presence of Jesus. Please choose *1 or 2 reflection responses* that you are drawn to. You can take time for this. You are worth it.

- What are the three biggest distractions that keep you from attuning to God's presence?

- Revisit a recent moment in your life and imagine what it might have looked like and felt like if you'd noticed God's presence and directed your attention to Him.

- Choose a day to fast from screens. Instead, carry a notebook with you and jot down every instance that makes you notice God. This is a great practice to include in a weekly Sabbath, too.

- List some practical ways you can be more present to God, your loved ones, and yourself today. Consider creating a physical reminder that will cue you to give your full attention to God and those around you.

59 Sacred Loveways

I SHOVE THE CASSEROLE IN the oven, glance at the clock *(forty-five minutes until I need to leave is enough time to make cookies, right?)*, and start scouring the internet for some magically-quick recipe so I can contribute a snack for my upcoming meeting.

Troy rolls in on his bicycle, plastic bags swinging from the handlebars. "Hey! Thanks for picking up fruit," I call out. He sees me slumped at the table, furrowing my brow at my phone, and asks what I'm doing. "I want to bring something to share tonight, but I don't really have time to make anything."

"How about mango? I just got a bunch." He watches for my relieved nod before grabbing a bowl and preparing the fruit. He even goes so far as to put plastic forks and cups in a bag. I make him swap the cups for plates. Who eats mango in a cup? It would work better, he says. I laugh. I admire his ability to think outside of the box. Even more than that, I admire how fluently he has learned to speak my love language: Acts of Service.

In case you're not familiar with the Five Love Languages[1], the core ways that Dr. Gary Chapman outlines as our primary modes for giving and receiving love are: Acts of Service, Receiving Gifts, Quality Time, Physical

Touch, and Words of Affirmation. You might prefer to *show* love in one way while you *receive* love in another; and, as in most profile types, you can have more than one love language. Go ahead and search it up. It's worth your time.

Every member of my family has a different love language. My husband's primary language is Words of Affirmation. My oldest son soaks up Quality Time, my daughter delights in Receiving Gifts, and my youngest son needs extra Physical Touch. Recognizing these differences in each other helps us connect more deeply and appreciate each other's unique way of showing love.

Love languages are a helpful model for human relationships, but can we stretch this idea into our relationship with God? I would dare to say, absolutely yes.

In the last chapter, we considered how God reveals his loving presence in our lives in ways that we can individually understand. But have you ever thought about the unique, specific, and deeply personal way *you* show love back to God? Or do you just go through the motions, parroting what you have been shown of a relationship with Jesus?

Like a child learning to speak, we all start with mimicry, but, at some point, we must learn to express ourselves personally to others and to God.

Another man named Gary—Gary Thomas—took this idea of individual modes of relating to God and developed something he calls Spiritual Temperaments. In his book,

Sacred Pathways: Nine Ways to Connect with God, he outlines a few of the examples found in the Bible.

"Scripture tells us that the same God is present from Genesis through Revelation—though people worshiped that one God in many ways: Abraham had a religious bent, building altars everywhere he went. Moses and Elijah revealed an activist's streak in their various confrontations with forces of evil and in their conversations with God. David celebrated God with an enthusiastic style of worship, while his son Solomon expressed his love for God by offering generous sacrifices. Ezekiel and John described loud and colorful images of God, stunning in sensuous brilliance. Mordecai demonstrated his love for God by caring for others, beginning with the orphaned Esther. Mary of Bethany is the classic contemplative, sitting at Jesus's feet."[2]

From these and other Christian writers and church movements throughout history, he defines the nine Spiritual Temperaments as: the Naturalist—let me be outdoors; the Sensate—let me experience; the Traditionalist—let me remember; the Ascetic—let me be alone; the Activist—let me conquer; the Caregiver—let me care; the Enthusiast—let me celebrate; the Contemplative—let me feel; and the Intellectual—let me think.

Again, it is well worth your time to read his book or at least search up these pathways.

"Ultimately, it's a matter of spiritual nutrition. . . what feeds one doesn't feed all. Giving the same spiritual prescription to every struggling Christian is no less irresponsible than a doctor prescribing penicillin to combat every illness," writes Gary. Are you feeding your relationship with Jesus the best foods, or are you stunting its growth with a limited menu?

What I've found as I've begun to approach my relationship with Father, Son, and Spirit through the lenses of Love Languages and Sacred Pathways is simply an incredible sense of *freedom* for both myself and in how I view others. One mode of connecting with Him is not inherently better or more spiritual than another. What I use to demonstrate my love and devotion to Jesus is my own unique gift to Him. And He accepts it as it is because He accepts me as I am.

I'm not talking about theological compromise or doctrinal fluffiness. The rock of God's Word stands firm, and we can't ignore reading the Bible just because we prefer to dance or light a candle or feed the hungry. But I do believe that often our idea of acceptable worship is too small. Perhaps because our view of God is too small.

He is worthy of worship from every tribe and tongue and people and nation.[3]

"For from Him and through Him and to Him are all things. To Him be the glory forever."[4]

"He is the King eternal, immortal, invisible, the only God."[5]

Living in a foreign country has allowed me to see different ways of thinking, connecting, and worshiping that I never imagined before. And it's beautiful. The diversity of the worship of the Lamb of God as He receives praise in countless different languages across the globe is glorious. The complexity of humans and the marvel of a God who can simultaneously and specifically connect with each of us absolutely floors me.

He is worthy.

And He longs for the truest love you have to offer Him—the love that comes most naturally out of the authentic you. The love He created you, and you alone, to share with Him.

If you've come to this book feeling stuck, weary, or dry, perhaps it's time to check how you've been feeding your soul through connection with Jesus. Consider how you enjoy offering love in your human relationships, and try worshiping God in that way—, perhaps with a gift, a love note, a hands-on service project, or a sunset stroll. Experiment with a new Sacred Pathway by going for a hike, reading liturgy, diving into an excellent sermon series, taking a silent retreat, doing street evangelism, imagining yourself in a Bible story, attending a live worship event, or setting up a specific devotional space filled with imagery, candles, and a fresh worship playlist.

As in any relationship, familiar interactions bring comfort, but shared new experiences stir excitement and create a depth of knowing that can't be experienced by visiting the same coffee shop and having the same conversation every day. Try something new with Jesus this week and see if it makes your soul come alive.

Catch the Rain

Here you are invited to open your heart in the presence of Jesus. Please choose *1 or 2 reflection responses* that you are drawn to. You can take time for this. You are worth it.

- Try to identify your dominant Love Language and Sacred Pathway. An internet search can provide a detailed summary of each.

- Which Bible story do you admire the most as an example of worship? How do your favorite teachers typically connect with God? This may indicate your spiritual temperament.

- Choose an expression of love for God that is out of the ordinary for you and try it. What does it do for your relationship with Jesus?

- Think of a few people who connect with God very differently from you. Do you need to view their worship with more respect? Can you learn something from them?

Part 4
HEART, SOUL, MIND AND STRENGTH

The Scriptures tell us, "Love your neighbor as yourself," but most of us never really learn to love ourselves, thinking we can make up for this deficit if we practice loving others. We have to practice what love is by making room for who we are—the good and the bad. Otherwise, the love we offer others will always lack the depth of its potential.

— Christopher L. Heuertz, *The Sacred Enneagram*[1]

KEY STEP:
BRING ALL OF YOU

In Part Four, you're going to look at everything from your schedule to your physical limitations to submit every last part of you into the Healer's tender care. As you move through this section, a key spiritual practice will be *embodied worship,* or praising and surrendering to God with your actual, beautifully-created-but-broken human body.

To practice embodied worship, you can try:

- Creating something that represents an attribute of God
- Raising your hands while singing
- Stretching while listening to scripture or reciting a memorized verse
- Taking regular prayer walks or runs
- Kneeling or lying prostrate when praying
- Dancing to worship music
- Eating well-balanced, low-sugar meals while giving specific thanks for each food
- Playing an instrument while worshiping
- Napping (Yes, this can be a spiritual discipline!)
- Visiting a health care specialist

Embodied Worship

TODAY I AM ANNOYINGLY AWARE of my body. Just to get to these words I have moved to the dining room table (the tall desk in my room just felt too, well, *tall* today), brought a pillow from the couch to go behind my back (these wooden chairs have no contour), settled in to write only to pop back up again to find some socks (who can write with cold toes?), munched on a bowl of tortilla chips while rereading the last chapter (salt cravings are real, my friend), and found about a dozen other environmental adjustments to make before finding the words for this incredibly long sentence.

Perhaps all this because I am delving into the practice of embodied worship today.

Or perhaps I'm just fussy.

Either way, I am clearly more than a mind doling out thoughts to entertain you. I am dependent on my fingers to type, my eyes to see what I've written, my achy back to support my frame, and my heart to keep the blood flowing through it all. This is me: the living, breathing Corella Roberts.

I consist of a regenerated spirit that will live for eternity with Christ, but also an earthly body that will someday become a resurrected, heavenly body. The two are intricately interwoven.

But are both spirit and body valued equally by God?

Therapist Aundi Kolber offers her thoughts: "Jesus came to show us the truest, best way to be human—not by denying His humanity but by embracing it. By living in it. By dying in it. And then, finally, by being resurrected in a glorified body. Jesus loves our humanity. And Jesus's life on earth is why we can confidently say that God values our flesh and bones."[1]

He values our flesh and bones so much that he was publicly humiliated and physically tortured that we might *also* have resurrected bodies. This can't be understated, though the implications of it are often ignored.

Jesus died to save my body.

Ever heard that one? Souls, yes, but bodies? Paul seems to suggest so in his letter to the church in Rome—a church comprised of people who freshly understood the transition from a life of bodily sin to a life of bodily worship. He writes, "We know that the whole creation has been groaning as in the pains of childbirth right up to the present time. Not only so, but we ourselves, who have the first fruits of the Spirit, groan inwardly as we wait eagerly for our adoption to sonship, the redemption of our bodies."[2]

How do we live out an embodied faith while we wait, groaning inwardly (sometimes outwardly, too), for the redemption of our bodies? And what does that look like in this healing journey we're on?

First of all, it's easier than we dare to think. Simple, physical acts such as bowing your head in reverence or gazing skyward in joy, moving to music or kneeling in silence, hugging a sad friend or crying our own tears in God's presence are all ways to integrate our faith with our bodies.

Sometimes, too, the mind is weak, or the heart is broken, and these expressions are all we have.

"In the midst of this, though words failed me, prayer without words—prayer in and through my body—became a lifeline. I couldn't find words, but I could kneel. I could submit to God through my knees, and I'd lift my hands to hold up an ache: a fleshy, unnamable longing that I carried around my ribs. I'd offer up an aching body with my hands, my knees, my tears, my lifted eyes. My body led in prayer and led me—all of me, eventually even my words—into prayer," shares author Tish Harrison Warren.[3]

Several years ago, a friend gripped my arm and said that God was asking her to do something scary. Would I please pray for her? Concerned, I agreed. And then, to the astonishment of the nearly one hundred other women in the room, my friend stood up and began to dance.

Through her beautiful Portuguese accent and a well of tears, she told us how she was born to dance. She loved it with every fiber of her being, but when she came to Christ, she was told it was sinful, so she stopped. She hid and shamed this gift of hers until that night, when she set it free in worship. Both the lyrics and her movements beckoned us to the throne room of the Lamb. *Alleluia, for the Lord God Almighty Reigns!*

Those of us present knew we were witnessing the healing of a soul. A foretaste to the redemption of a body. It was beyond beautiful. We all wept, and then something equally miraculous happened: several other women began dancing, too. Their motions, graceful or otherwise, swept around the room with the purity of a daughter twirling in her daddy's arms.

Embodied worship. The healing of a soul. The delight of the Father.

Burnout affects more than just your mind or your emotions, and it's no secret that stress and exhaustion take their toll on your whole being. Therefore, your soul restoration practices *must* include your body.

I'm no doctor, so if you have serious physical concerns, please see one, but I would like to offer some basic suggestions for living an embodied faith that fosters soul healing.

Worship. Lift your voice, raise your hands, lay face down, clap, dance, play an instrument—however you like to praise God, engage your whole self in it. If this is awkward or uncomfortable for you in your church setting, do it alone. You'll know, like my friend did, if God is urging you to bring freedom to others by doing it in public. But for now, get your own heart, mind, *and* body fully engaged in praising God. After all, it is what you were created to do; worship is coming home for the human soul.

Rest. A life filled with stress, demands, frustrations, and heavy responsibility is often a body flooded with cortisol, aka the stress hormone. And, you may not want to hear this, but the number one way to lower those cortisol levels is to get enough sleep.[4] Getting out in nature and moving your body gently by hiking, walking, or biking are helpful, too. Meditating on scripture, especially when paired with slow, deep breathing, is an excellent, integrated way to reduce stress. Try this one: Breathe in slowly while thinking *"Peace of Christ"* then breathe out slowly while thinking *"Guard my heart."* Also high on the list are laughter, a whole-foods diet (think lots of fruits and veggies and very limited sugar and processed snacks), and quality time with loved ones.

Exercise. Slow, moderate exercise is wonderful for lowering cortisol levels, but a more rigorous exercise routine can help you sleep better, boost your mood, improve your heart health, and strengthen your muscles.[5] Remember, we're not doing these activities out of vanity; rather, we're desiring to honor God with our bodies and trust that He cares for our whole selves.

115

Create. We are crafted in the image of a creative God. He has hard-wired creativity into our DNA, and exercising your creative gifts is a sure path toward healing. Maybe you create meaning with words, paint, melody, or clay. Maybe you create beauty through gardening, photography, woodworking, or sewing. Maybe you create order through organized drawers, spreadsheets, or lesson plans. Or maybe you create sustenance through cooking and baking. Our endless God has given us endless modes to reflect His creativity. Which one has He given to you?

Now, two days after beginning this chapter while restless at home, I end it at a quiet café tucked in the hills of Northern Thailand. A fan cools my back, a Thai milk tea soothes my throat, and out the window I watch leaf-sized birds dance from one flowered tree branch to another. Beyond them, a breeze stirs the verdant hillside and heavy clouds spill over the mountains on the horizon. I feel refreshed from my earlier workout and shower, and here, in this space, the words flow freely. The simple contentment of this moment for my mind, heart, and body is tangible.

As it should be.

Catch the Rain

Here you are invited to open your heart in the presence of Jesus. Please choose *1 or 2 reflection responses* that you are drawn to. You can take time for this. You are worth it.

- Read Psalm 63. List the body parts that David incorporates in this prayer. What parts of you physically ache for the fullness of God?

- Be brave and experiment with wordless prayer through movement or dance. Simply play a meaningful song and let your body cry out to God through it. What did this experience do in you?

- Which of the practices mentioned for worship, rest, exercise, or creativity feel like an invitation for you? What steps will you take to begin?

- Describe a time that you felt at peace and connected to God in both body and spirit. What facilitated that moment of integrated faith?

A Living Temple

A FEW YEARS AGO, I became convinced that I needed a more substantial morning quiet time before the kids woke up. That meant I'd have to get up no later than 5:30am to squeeze in maybe half an hour before my toddler rose with the sun. And that meant that I'd need to be asleep by 9:30pm to get eight hours of sleep.

I learned a few things about myself during the month or so that I somewhat pulled off this early morning time with God. One, I'm really bad at getting to bed early. Two, I'm not as disciplined as I'd like to think, and springing to life with the alarm clock's first ring is hard. Three, kids have a magical mommy-radar; the earlier I get up, the earlier they get up. And four, my morning quiet time didn't produce the glowingly peaceful spirit that I dreamed it would.

Instead, I became more irritable and selfish.

I wasn't getting enough sleep, and it caught up to me. More than that, though, was the reality that I hadn't correctly discerned my season and my spiritual need. I thought I needed more Bible study, so my mornings consisted of rapid scripture reading with commentary and the hopes to get through the Bible in a year.

You see, I want to be a hard-core missionary. I want to rise early to pray for an hour with Eric Liddell regardless of how hard I worked the day before or what the day ahead will hold.[1] I want to shrug off all that is safe and familiar and sleep in a hut next to Elisabeth Elliot, brushing snakes off my sleeping children as if it's nothing.[2] I want to pour out relentlessly, loving and teaching and living among the poorest of the poor with Mother Teresa.[3]

Their examples tell me it's possible. So why does it seem so impossible for me?

Perhaps it's one of those *what is impossible with man is possible with God* things. Or perhaps none of those shining examples could have looked at their end from their beginning and believed it possible either. Perhaps what we see from their lives is a composite of day by day, minute by minute choices to obey Christ. To dig deep into their unique God-given design—to be fast, and strong-willed, and compassionate—and choose to reflect that facet of Jesus a little bit more each day.

Each one, a living temple of the Spirit of God.

Looking back on that season of mothering young ones in a foreign country, I don't think I needed more head knowledge *of* God. I think I needed to be held *by* God, comforted and reassured the way I spent so many hours each day doing for my little ones. At the time, I had no idea what that looked like, but I did know that skimping sleep to study the Word was not working.

After a few weeks, I went back to eking out every spare minute of sleep I could and reading a smaller dose of scripture each afternoon when the kids were resting in their rooms. The result?

I was more Jesus-like.

I had more patience. I gave myself, and therefore others, more grace. I wasn't resentful of my children for "stealing" my time with God when they woke up earlier than normal. I had more time with my husband in the evenings after putting the kids to bed. And I found I was actually in a better space mentally and physically to absorb God's Word in those afternoon moments.

In that place of failure, of weakness, I found God's strength. In humbly meeting God within the limits of my season, I somehow made more space for His presence. I honored my body as a living temple of the Holy Spirit.

You are a living temple, too. A soul *within*, not separate from, a body. Jesus doesn't just live in this little box we like to call your "heart." He makes His home in *all* of you. Every last bit of your mind and affections and will and body, indwelt by the living God.

This presupposes, of course, a surrendered life. An undivided heart. A willingness to love Jesus with heart, soul, mind, and strength.

The next thought, then, is not such a far leap: If we can love Him like that, then, surely, we can serve Him like the "great ones," right?

But what, then, of the brokenhearted? The soul-sick? The mentally ill? The physically weary? Is there a place for us at God's table? In His list of faithful saints?

My Grandpa Levig was a tough-as-nails Norwegian whose favorite things included driving a tractor, lefsa, fishing, and the word "uff-da." He and my grandma spent a couple of years in Tanzania where he used his practical skills to improve the community's quality of life. This is what he loved—helping people with his hands.

As he grew older, those overseas trips were no longer possible and much of the manual labor of the tree nursery he owned was passed on to younger, stronger hands. Yet, in his later years, he found an unexpected way to physically help others. He learned to sew quilts. He spent hours and hours patching little squares together to pass on to a team who would back them and fill them. Then, they'd ship them to Africa. He was still going to the place he loved through those quilts—hundreds of them.

He didn't let his weakness stop him from serving. But he did acknowledge it and adapt to it.

More often than not, ignoring our physical, mental, and emotional limitations is just plain ol' pride. We want to be more than we are. We want to be limitless. We want to be God.

I don't believe it was pride that produced the constancy of devotion we saw in Eric Liddell, the steadfast faith we saw in Elisabeth Elliot, or the sacrificial service we saw in Mother Teresa. No, their lives look more like a picture of trust to me.

Trust that Christ was, is, and ever will be enough. More than enough. Even in—especially in—their weakness. They showed up every day with the conviction to do whatever Jesus asked of them, no more, no less.

Sometimes—oftentimes—God asks us to do hard things. He calls us to persevere. I don't mean to imply that faithfully finishing a difficult task or season is pride, and I also don't mean to say that giving in to physical indulgence is trust. I hope you're hearing throughout these pages that we need the Spirit's discernment for when to push through and when to pull back, and the only way to tell the difference is to slow down long enough to hear His voice. Listening to His Word, the counsel of a friend, His still, small voice, and even your own body, is a radical act of trust.

When I ask you to bring all of you, I mean the broken parts, too. You show up with your chronic fatigue, your anxiety, your arthritis, your wounded past, your dyslexia, your thyroid issues, your eczema, your burnout, and your insurmountable need for eight hours of sleep a night, and He will meet you with his tenderhearted grace and all-sufficient strength.

In fact, Jesus will call you blessed:

You're blessed when you're at the end of your rope. With less of you there is more of God and his rule.

You're blessed when you feel you've lost what is most dear to you. Only then can you be embraced by the One most dear to you.

You're blessed when you're content with just who you are—no more, no less. That's the moment you find yourselves proud owners of everything that can't be bought.

You're blessed when you've worked up a good appetite for God. He's food and drink in the best meal you'll ever eat.

You're blessed when you care. At the moment of being 'care-full,' you find yourselves cared for.

You're blessed when you get your inside world— your mind and heart—put right. Then you can see God in the outside world.

You're blessed when you can show people how to cooperate instead of compete or fight. That's when you discover who you really are, and your place in God's family.

124

You're blessed when your commitment to God provokes persecution. The persecution drives you even deeper into God's kingdom. (Matthew 5:3–10 MSG)

Our experience of God is richer, fuller, when our experience of life is broken, humbled. So, what are your weaknesses? And have you been trusting God's strength to meet you in them?

You are a living temple of the Holy Spirit. And you— every last fractured and scuffed and scarred piece of you—is beautiful because of it.

Catch the Rain

Here you are invited to open your heart in the presence of Jesus. Please choose *1 or 2 reflection responses* that you are drawn to. You can take time for this. You are worth it.

⬩ Think of a time you extended yourself beyond your physical, mental, or emotional limits. What was the outcome? Were you able to follow that output with a time of replenishment?

⬩ Are there specific parts of you that are hard to envision as indwelt and loved by the Holy Spirit? Why do you think that is? Have a conversation with God (and preferably a friend, too!) about it.

⬩ What area is in the most need of renewal in your life? Consider sleeping and eating habits, stress load, relational wellness, and mental strain. Invite Jesus into that area and pray about a first step to take toward healing in it.

⬩ Meditate on the Beatitudes every day for one week. (Matthew 5:1–12)

System Reboot

I THINK I'VE BEEN LATE to the game in a few life basics. The enjoyment of coffee, for one, and the use of a meal plan, for two. I can say, though, that I have finally developed both of those things in my late thirties. The ability to appreciate coffee is nice in social settings where I get to feel like a real adult, and the weekly meal plan is bringing newfound freedom from that ever-haunting question of *What will we eat tonight?*, which is probably the more important of the two.

Meatless Mondays, Taco Tuesdays, and Simple Saturdays, which incorporate kid-faves like grilled cheese and tuna sandwiches, are some of the themes that I use to guide the big picture of my meal plan. (The other days aren't alliterative and, therefore, not worth mentioning.) I sit down at the beginning of the month with a calendar that hangs on the fridge, and I plug our favorites and a few new Pinterest recipes into each day. Now I know what to shop for when I go to the grocery store. I cross each day off as I prepare that meal, and that way, if we end up eating out with friends or just working through leftovers instead, I can look back later at the meals I didn't make and maybe swap it for a day I'm less excited about.

I'm telling you all this because having a meal planning system has simplified my life. In a very real way, it has reduced stress, allowed me more time, and increased the amount of healthy foods we consume. (Fewer chicken nuggets is generally a win.) And often in our lives, there is an area that needs a meal plan, of sorts—something to create structure and eliminate making decisions under pressure.

Kendra Adachi, author of *The Lazy Genius Way: Embrace What Matters, Ditch what Doesn't, and Get Stuff Done*, is, well, genius at this. She suggests, "Name something that stresses you out, and make one decision to make it easier. One, not thirty-seven."[1]

If you do not start small and stay consistent, nothing will change. So, what is one part of your life that could use a system reboot?

About fifteen years into marriage, Troy and I realized that we don't do conversations well at night. (See? Late to the game.) When we finally get the kids in bed and the house straightened, our minds turn to the next day, and we clarify plans and expectations. This mostly works, but when we need to plan further ahead or hash through emotional decisions, nighttime talks are a recipe for disaster. Misunderstandings, hurt feelings, impatience, and even dozing off in the middle of a discussion are not uncommon.

One day, Troy offered to block out two hours of his morning schedule once a week so we could spend time together talking and praying. Honestly, I resisted at first. *I don't want to take your time. People at school need you. What if you let other meetings run over it and I just feel disappointed again?* But he promised to guard that time and suggested we try it for one month. Now, two years later, we are most definitely more connected and joyful in our marriage because of it. I'll say it here in writing (just this once): You were right, Love.

Deciding what to make for dinner was a constant nuisance. My one change: create a meal plan.

Nighttime conversations with my husband were creating conflict. My one change: make time for a weekly morning connection.

These are practical pieces of life. And they matter. You do not have to have a meal plan or weekly morning dates with your spouse, but what *do* you need? What's the one area causing stress or discord? If it's your finances, consider setting up a budget. If it's family scheduling with multiple members involved in a variety of activities, try using a shared calendar app. If it's a nagging physical concern, try making one concrete change to your diet or exercise for a month and see how you feel.

One thing. Not thirty-seven.

Here's Kendra, again, to remind us in her genius way of where we're *not* going with all of this. "Does everyone else have this figured out?. . . One person can't possibly keep up with a clean house, a fulfilling job, a well-adjusted family, an active social life, and a running regimen of fifteen miles a week, right? With silence our only answer, we decide, No, it's just me. I need to get it together. What follows is a flurry of habit trackers, calendar overhauls, and internet rabbit holes to figure out how to be better, until we pass out from emotional exhaustion or actual adrenal fatigue or we give up completely."[2]

We're *not* talking about doing tricks to become more efficient so we can do it all and then some. We *are* talking about making wise decisions to simplify everyday life and reduce unnecessary stress. We're talking about identifying places that need some love so they can nurture and not drain us. We're talking about asking God for help in even the littlest things, thereby declaring radical trust and intimate friendship with Him.

Let's spend a few moments with Jesus here. Come on over to this grassy knoll and have a seat next to me. There are hundreds of others tucked onto this hillside, matting down the tall grass, accidentally tromping on the flowers. The sun is dipping low, its rays splashing off the Sea of Galilee in golden ripples as swallows skim across the surface, gobbling up their evening meal. And just above us, the Teacher sits. He's been at it for a while, but His voice holds steady, unwavering in authority and peace.

No one can serve two masters. Either you will hate the one and love the other, or you will be devoted to the

*one and despise the other. You cannot serve both God
and money.*

*Therefore I tell you, do not worry about your life, what
you will eat or drink; or about your body, what you
will wear. Is not life more than food, and the body
more than clothes? Look at the birds of the air; they do
not sow or reap or store away in barns, and yet your
heavenly Father feeds them. Are you not much more
valuable than they? Can any one of you by worrying
add a single hour to your life?* (Matthew 6:24–27)

At the mention of worry, does a picture come to mind?
Images of that familiar struggle? What would the Teacher
say if you told Him about it? Would He dismiss it as un-
important? Surely not, for He cares for you.[3] Would He
tell you to man up, try harder, soldier on? Unlikely, for
He invites the weary and burdened to come to Him for
rest.[4] What *would* He say? What *does* He say?

You are no longer one of hundreds or thousands clam-
oring to be near Him. The Teacher sits alone with you,
offering undivided attention. What do you want to tell
Him today?

Catch the Rain

Here you are invited to open your heart in the presence of Jesus. Please choose *1 or 2 reflection responses* that you are drawn to. You can take time for this. You are worth it.

- Journal your conversation with Jesus, the Teacher, about what is worrying you. Does He offer a wise solution to that particular stressor in your life?

- What areas of your life already have a system, or a rhythm, that is helping them run smoothly? Think about how you got started with those systems and celebrate their success.

- What is the one change you want to try in order to reduce worry, stress, or discord? Tell it to a friend who can keep you accountable.

- If you feel stuck in a particular area of frustration, who can you go to for advice or even help to get started? Schedule a time to meet with that person.

A Consuming Love

IF YOU HAVEN'T NOTICED by now, I believe strongly that there is a solid link between the first and greatest commandment—to love the Lord your God with all your heart, soul, mind and strength—and the second—to love your neighbor as yourself. It's precisely in this holistic, embodied, all-consuming love for God that we discover His holistic, embodied, all-consuming love for us, thereby enabling us to also love ourselves and others.

All too often, as we come to a place in our journey where we try all the worship styles and schedule changes and stress management techniques, and we still can't get past that deep, dark, underlying voice. You know. The one that says you'll never be enough. Or you're unlovable. Or your only value is in what you accomplish. Or no one really sees or cares about you. Or you're the only one you can really depend on. Or . . .

These are lies and they are aimed straight at your sense of worth. If they are not uprooted and replaced with tenacious truth, you will find yourself back in the same struggles disguised in a different shape, time and time again.

Chances are, I'm telling you nothing new. You know your recurring battles. You might even know the false narrative that you keep believing (although many of us don't). But do you know how to swim up from under it and breathe the air of freedom?

For a long time, I thought I did. Turns out, though, that I couldn't recognize the counterfeit until I'd really seen the truth. Let me tell you about my word. The one I have emblazoned over my heart indelibly. My tattoo.

It was nearing my thirty-fifth birthday and what was about to be the pinnacle (although I didn't know it then) of my two-year journey back to God's heart after an intense wilderness season. A friend had gifted me a Bible in a new translation[1] and insisted that I read the Song of Songs in it.

I knew what the Song of Songs was about. Troy and I had gone through a premarital course on it, and I thought maybe she wanted to encourage us to reignite that romantic spark of complimenting each other's hair like the goats of Gilead and bellies like a heap of wheat. I mean, who couldn't use that inspiration, right?

But as I began reading, I found I was captivated by the back and forth of the bridegroom and the bride. Her expressions of love were all over the place, one minute throwing herself at the man, the next hiding from him; exulting in his love, then declaring herself unworthy of his attention. This, I thought, is an honest picture of my heart. Yet, the bridegroom is unwavering in his expressions of her beauty and worth, and of his invitational love. This, I thought, is the perfect picture of Jesus.

Intrigued, I studied further and found that while modern Christianity has often pushed this book aside as either romantic poetry or, at best, a testimony to the beauty of sensual love within marriage, Jews have regarded it throughout the ages as a sacred allegory of God's love for His people. It is, in fact, even commonly read during the week leading up to Passover (what we refer to as Passion Week).[2]

Could God's love for me really be as fierce, relentless, generous, devout, and intense as the bridegroom's love? Could He possibly deign to say to me:

> *How beautiful you are, my darling!*
> *Oh, how beautiful!*
> *Your eyes are doves. . .*
>
> *Arise, my darling, my beautiful one,*
> *And come along.*
> *For behold, the winter is past,*
> *The rain is over and gone. . .*
>
> *How beautiful is your love, my sister, my bride!*
> *How much sweeter is your love than wine,*
> *And the fragrance of your oils*
> *Than that of all kinds of balsam oils!* (Song 1:15, 2:10–11, 4:10 NASB)

The thought of it leaves me undone.

As I read to the end of Song of Songs, I found the encapsulation of this unquenchable love.

> *Put me like a seal over your heart,*
> *Like a seal on your arm.*
> *For love is as strong as death,*
> *Jealousy is as severe as Sheol;*
> *Its flames are flames of fire,*
> *The flame of the Lord.* (Song 8:6 NASB)

My Bible's footnote pointed out that the phrase "the flame of the Lord" was from two Hebrew words: *shelhebet* and *Yah.* The first part meaning a mighty flash of fire, the second being the very name of God. In other words, the love of the Almighty God is as fierce as the very flames emanating from His presence.

Could it be that there is no distinction, no separation, between God's holiness and His love? Consider Ezekiel 1 where the Lord Himself is described like "gleaming metal that looked like fire all around within it, and from the appearance of His waist and downward I saw something like fire; and there was a radiance around Him" (v. 27). Or Revelation 4 where "out from the throne came flashes of lightning and sounds and peals of thunder" (v. 5). Or the appearance of the Son of Man in Revelation 1, when John saw that "His eyes were like a flame of fire. His feet were like burnished bronze when it has been heated to a glow in a furnace, and His voice was like the sound of many waters. In His right hand He held seven stars, and out of His mouth came a sharp two-edged sword; and His face was like the sun shining in its strength" (vv. 14–16).

If the very radiance of the Lord is *shelhebet*—a most vehement flame, then Song of Songs 8:6 is calling what emanates from Him, love. And because He is holy, that love is perfect. Somehow—only through the blood of Christ—that perfectly holy love is aimed at me.

Right then and there, I made a rather impulsive decision to take that verse literally and place a declaration of his love as a seal over my heart. A few days later, with the support of three friends as crazy as I am, I walked out of a tattoo parlor with *shelhebet-Yah* forever stamped on my chest.

This, the all-consuming, flaming love of my Creator is my defining mark.

My worth, my security, my lovableness, my beauty are not given to me by any other than Yahweh. He alone tells me how important and valuable I am. No one and nothing else has that right. That's what *shelhebet-Yah* will forever remind me.

And it wasn't until I saw the lies I'd been believing against the dazzling brightness of the truth that I recognized them for what they really were. And I cast them into the fire of His love.

Catch the Rain

Here you are invited to open your heart in the presence of Jesus. Please choose *1 or 2 reflection responses* that intrigue you. You can take time for this. You are worth it.

- Read through the entirety of Song of Songs in one sitting. What do you find beautiful in it? What do you have resistance to? What do you long for?

- Which self-worth lie triggers you the most often?
  - I'll never be enough.
  - I'm unlovable.
  - My only value is in what I accomplish.
  - No one really sees or cares about me.
  - I'm the only one I can really depend on.
  Face that lie head-on and ask Jesus for a deep revelation of the truth He wants to replace it with.

- Find a word or image to remind you of the truth you most need to embrace and live from, then create a physical reminder with that word/image (such as a bookmark, lock screen, or painting).

Part 5
NOT ON MY OWN

Wrong will be right,

when Aslan comes in sight,

At the sound of his roar,

sorrows will be no more,

When he bares his teeth,

winter meets its death,

And when he shakes his mane,

we shall have spring again.

— C.S. Lewis, *The Lion, The Witch and the Wardrobe*[1]

KEY STEP:
LET GOD FIGHT FOR YOU

In Part Five, you'll be encouraged to trust the nearness, authority, and protection of Christ in ever-deepening ways. If you haven't already been writing down your journey with the Lord, I'd like to encourage you to begin the practice of *journaling*.

To be honest, as much as I like to write, I often find it a struggle to journal. However, handwriting our experiences, prayers, reflections, and meaningful scriptures strengthens them in two ways. One, we remember better what we physically write. And two, there is a record to look back on for meaningful reflection later. Here are a few thoughts that have kept this reluctant journaler going:

- Literally journal *anything*—one word to summarize the day, a quote from a book, a doodle, a prayer, a dream, an idea. . . This doesn't have to be a "Dear Diary" format.
- Use a notebook and pen/pencil you love
- Schedule time for it at least weekly
- Give yourself a set question to answer (i.e. How did I notice God with me today?)

Courage, Dear Heart

I AM AN UNASHAMED C.S. LEWIS fan. It's not because he's a talented writer, although he is. It's not because he's a brilliant theologian, although he's that, too. I love the works of Lewis because he brings heavenly realities so near that I feel as though I could touch them through the mane of a lion or the cold metal of a lamppost. If you haven't read *The Chronicles of Narnia* as an adult, just set this book aside and go do that right now.

Through Aslan, the lion character that is a portrayal of Jesus, C.S. Lewis reminds us of Christ's undeniable strength and kingship right alongside His compassion and goodness. I get goosebumps every time I read of Aslan singing creation into being or roaring a battle cry after his resurrection, all while children witness his power and then are invited to ride on his back. It's no surprise that the youngest child in the scene, Lucy, has the sweetest and closest relationship with Aslan.

A favorite quote of many comes from *The Voyage of the Dawn Treader*: "But no one but Lucy knew that as [the albatross] circled the mast it had whispered to her, 'Courage, dear heart,' and the voice, she felt sure, was Aslan's, and with the voice a delicious smell breathed in her face."[1]

Courage, dear heart. Don't we all need that whispered in our ear as we face life's battles and sorrows? More than that, we need the fresh breath of the Holy Spirit to empower us to *have* courage. To stand firm. To face the storm.

We all need to know that we are not alone.

Some of the loneliest days of my life have been spent mothering littles while living overseas. No family to fall back on for support. No long-standing network of friends (sadly, many move away after a year or two). No familiar aisles of baby food or products at the store. No well-known pediatrician. No amazing childcare at church. No ease of communication for help with the most basic tasks. You get the idea.

I remember one day when my daughter, just a toddler then, had a fever. Her energetic, preschool-aged brother was feeling more than fine and up to his usual antics. Troy was at work and I had no grandparents or aunties to call on, so I decided we needed to get out of the house. But where could I go with a sick child? I saw my bicycle with a baby basket between the handlebars and my son's small bike parked next to it. *I guess that will have to do*, I thought as I plunked my lethargic, whimpering child in the basket and headed out to do laps around the neighborhood.

I could begrudge my independent, go-getter personality that, combined with my trust in God, landed me here in the middle of Lonely Motherville, Thailand.

But, honestly, I don't regret it one bit.

In the absence of many familiar comforts, I've had to seek the nearness of Jesus. I've had to cry out to him for wisdom. I've had to grab hold of his lion's mane and feel his strength to get me through the day.

Courage, dear heart.

Perhaps the second loneliest experience I've known has been stepping into the world of writing. Without a friend to guide me or a group to go with me, I one day decided to share my words with whoever would read them, claiming the title of author. It's a highly misunderstood label, I'm learning. And it necessitates a slew of skill sets beyond mere wordsmithing: marketing, graphic design, and networking to name a few. New and scary places for me to dip my toes. Yet, I can't deny that I hear the whisper every time I sit down to write: Courage, dear heart.

I know that while mothering, writing, standing out as a foreigner, and sharing my faith can feel lonely, I am not alone. The Lion of the Tribe of Judah[2] stands with me. Sometimes He goes before me, clearing the way with a roar. Sometimes He stands behind me, nudging me forward, giving me His strength to lean back on. But He is always with me. Holding this Aslan-type imagery near has helped me in many uncertain situations.

Perhaps a different picture from Zechariah 2:4 might capture your imagination. "'And I myself will be a wall of fire around it,' declares the Lord, 'and I will be its glory within.'" This is a message from an angel to Zechariah announcing the full and protective presence of God that will one day dwell with His people. Hasn't that always been the promise and the deepest yearning of our hearts? The very presence of God? The prophets wrote about instances when enemy city walls were destroyed by fire; yet here, the wall around Jerusalem *is* a fire. A consuming fire. *Shelhebet-Yah*, perhaps? And we, the people of God, are on the inside of it. More than that, He is the glory within us. It's no coincidence that the Holy Spirit came as tongues of fire.[3] He is protection and strength both without and within.

Similarly, God's angels encamp around us with chariots of fire: "And Elisha prayed, 'Open his eyes, Lord, so that he may see.' Then the Lord opened the servant's eyes, and he looked and saw the hills full of horses and chariots of fire all around Elisha." (2 Kings 6:17)

Maybe our eyes need to be opened and our imaginations redeemed. What if we're seeing it all wrong and this fleeting life is the dream while heaven is the reality? We're walking in what C.S. Lewis calls the Shadowlands. One day we will experience life in full radiance unlike anything we can imagine. "Heaven is reality itself. All that is fully real is Heavenly. For all that can be shaken will be shaken and only the unshakeable remains."[4] How would grasping that truth change our day-to-day perceptions and actions? What would that do to our fears?

Many of us are weary from the fight. But remember: the battle belongs to the Lord. Courage, dear heart. Whatever your struggle, you do not face it alone. The Lion of the Tribe of Judah is by your side. More than that, you are part of His body. The Spirit gives us unity—longs, even, to make us one.

The day of the feverish bike trip reminds me of this. Our neighborhood circuit took us past a friend's house whose son heard the rattling training wheels of my son's bicycle and ran outside. We paused to greet him, and soon his mother joined us. She frowned in concern as she felt the heat of my daughter's forehead.

"Chanan can stay here to play so you can take Rinnah home to rest," she insisted. I gratefully accepted and found in that moment the dual gift of His Spirit—comfort within and community without.

You have listened to fears, Child. . . Come, let me breathe on you. Forget them. Are you brave again?
—Aslan[5]

Again Jesus said, 'Peace be with you! As the Father has sent me, I am sending you.' And with that he breathed on them and said, 'Receive the Holy Spirit.'
—John 20:21–22

CATCH THE RAIN

Catch the Rain

Here you are invited to open your heart in the presence of Jesus. Please choose *1 or 2 reflection responses* that you are drawn to. You can take time for this. You are worth it.

- Which imagery resonates with you as you picture Jesus as your protector? The Lion, the wall of fire, or something else?

- Bring your fears to God and ask Him to open your eyes. Write down the spiritual realities He shows you.

- When and where do you tend to feel most alone? How can you remind yourself at those times that the Holy Spirit is with you?

- Read Psalm 46. Note the imagery of God as our fortress. What else stands out to you from this psalm?

Ultimate Authority

I HAVE A LOT OF STORIES from our seven years in bush Alaska. Some are cringe-worthy, others are tear-jerkers, and a few are just plain unbelievable (in fact, the whole experience necessitated a book[1]). But to this day, one of my favorites is fondly remembered as the "bear story."

One fall, Troy and I, my visiting parents, and two friends from our village attended a weekend camp in another small town. The first night after dinner and worship, we prepared to walk the quarter mile back to our guest-house—in the dark. None of us had thought to bring a flashlight. My dad joked about being prepared for bears by sticking a rock in his pocket, and we decided to sing along the way so we wouldn't startle any creatures on the unlit path.

We walked, huddled together, lifting our voices in an awkward rendition of "Jesus, All for Jesus" when a large, furry blur ran across the road just in front of us. Our singing suddenly turned into a chorus of screaming, rebuking, and barking. A rock launched into the darkness.

After a minute of frozen fear, we realized the bear was likely long gone and we hurried our way to the cabin. As we emerged from the dark, wooded path into the warmth of the porch light, our fear dissipated, and we began to chuckle as recognition of what had just happened swept over us. We recounted each of our reactions and laughed all the harder. I had screamed, "Bear!" and clung to Troy's arm. Troy had started barking like a dog. My mom rebuked the bear in the name of Yeshua while my dad threw his pathetically small rock. Our friend held out his Bible in front of him like a shield, and his wife ran to the back of the group to hide behind the rest of us.

Those hysterical reactions of fear gave us some wonderful ammunition for picking on each other for the rest of the weekend. And they said something about each of us and what we rely on in a moment of panic. It was a revealing experience in the most hilarious of ways.

My go-to was to sound the alarm and cling to someone stronger than me. And I've since realized that for most of my Christian life, that's how I've approached spiritual warfare, too.

As a little girl, I had frequent nightmares. I learned to call on the name of Jesus and sing praise songs to calm my fears and remind me of God's strength. Later as an adult, I occasionally had dreams that were outright demonic. In these dreams I would encounter an evil presence, try to cry out to Jesus for help, but be smothered and choked by an oppressive darkness until I awoke, heart racing. I would whisper the name of Jesus into the night and cling to His strength and power.

A few years ago, however, something shifted. I had a dream where I descended the stairs of a large house, opened the door at the bottom, and was immediately overwhelmed by the presence of evil. Fear threatened to choke me again, but this time, I stayed in the dream and managed to say, feebly at first, "Jesus Christ, King of kings and Lord of lords." Then I said it louder. Louder. Louder. Until the darkness fled. The dream continued as I explored the house further before returning to the original basement room. This time when I opened the door, the room was filled with children, laughter, and light.

Since then, I haven't had another dream where I was strangled by the fear of evil.

My mom may have been spot on when she rebuked that poor bear in the name of Yeshua (the Hebrew pronunciation of Jesus). His authority stands on its own. No rocks, dogs, or human strength necessary.

Jesus Christ, King of kings and Lord of lords.

The title comes from Revelation 17:14: "They will wage war against the Lamb, but the Lamb will triumph over them because he is Lord of lords and King of kings."

I love the clear truth Darrell W. Johnson points out about this passage when he writes, "So [the kings] go to war against him. But the Lamb wins. Why? Simply because of who he is. . . The war ends simply by Jesus Christ showing up. He wins because, although the seven heads and seven horns have great authority and strength, Jesus the Lamb has greater authority and strength."[2]

CATCH THE RAIN

Jesus Christ, King of kings and Lord of lords.

We encounter the designation again in the final battle against the beast, the false prophet, and the kings of the earth who have all gathered to wage war against Jesus, who is this time depicted not as a Lamb but as a warrior:

> *I saw heaven standing open and there before me was a white horse, whose rider is called Faithful and True. . . On his robe and on his thigh he has this name written:* KING OF KINGS AND LORD OF LORDS.
> (Revelation 19:11,16)

Then, almost as an unnecessary summary of the obvious conclusion to this battle "the beast was captured, and with it the false prophet who had performed the signs on its behalf. . . . The two of them were thrown alive into the fiery lake of burning sulfur" (Rev 19:20).

The battle is finished before it even begins. The King of kings and Lord of lords stands undefeated. Unharmed by the powers of sin, death, and every form of evil. Nothing rivals the authority of the Lamb.

If this is the outcome of the final battle, then is it not the outcome of every spiritual battle leading up to it? Even the places that at first look like defeat are only seeds buried in the ground, awaiting new life. The night awaiting the dawn. The cross awaiting the resurrection. Jesus is the light of life, and He always comes.

Life in this world isn't easy. It's not meant to be. We walk outside the garden where thorns tear our feet, and sweaty toil amidst conflict is the way of man. But that's not where the story ends. If we stay a little longer in Revelation, we come to a new garden set in a new city. And there, in the light of the King of kings and Lord of lords, we will drink of the river of life.

Then the angel showed me the river of the water of life, as clear as crystal, flowing from the throne of God and of the Lamb down the middle of the great street of the city. On each side of the river stood the tree of life, bearing twelve crops of fruit, yielding its fruit every month. And the leaves of the tree are for the healing of the nations. No longer will there be any curse. The throne of God and of the Lamb will be in the city, and his servants will serve him. They will see his face, and his name will be on their foreheads. There will be no more night. They will not need the light of a lamp or the light of the sun, for the Lord God will give them light. And they will reign for ever and ever. (Revelation 22:1–5)

In His presence, at His river, we won't even need to catch the rain.

153

Besides the incredible authority and power of Jesus, there is a reference in each of these passages to *us,* His disciples. In chapter 17, we're mentioned as His "called, chosen and faithful followers." In 19, the armies of the redeemed ride with Him. And in 22, it's His servants who see His face, receive His name and reign with Him for ever and ever.

I can't fathom why, but the undisputed King of the universe wants His creation to rule with Him. He wants to share His victory. His power. His authority. He is the ever-inviting God whose goodness, love, and justice overflowed into our souls when He breathed life into our bones. We're made for this. Made to be kings and queens, priests, and coheirs with Christ.

Not only can we face our battles knowing there is victory ahead, we can also stand in them with the authority of Christ. There is no need to be choked by fear anymore. Jesus Christ is King of kings and Lord of lords. And you are his child.

Catch the Rain

Here you are invited to open your heart in the presence of Jesus. Please choose *1 or 2 reflection responses* that you are drawn to. You can take time for this. You are worth it.

- Think of a time you were afraid. What was your automatic response? What does this reveal about your past experiences and where you place your trust?

- List the battles you are currently fighting (any regular struggle that you want to overcome). Now, with a broad marker or paint, write in large letters over the top of the list: JESUS IS KING OF KINGS AND LORD OF LORDS. Keep this as a reminder to trust His authority and to pray for His victory to come in His way.

- Read Exodus 14 and spend time meditating on verses 13 and 14. What might it look like in your life to be still and watch the Lord fight for you?

- Perhaps over the last two chapters God has revealed a bit of the spiritual reality behind a fear or battle you face. Find a pastor or friend who walks

in the authority of Christ and ask them to pray
with you and over you for freedom and hope.

The Dream Keeper

FINDING MY WAY BACK TO the Father's heart for me after wearing myself out in service to Him has been an interesting journey. One unexpected twist after another has brought me here, to these pages. My seven-year-old self, delighted by an award from a Young Author's Contest, believed this day would come. But somewhere in the journey of surrender, I lost the dream. The anticipation. The hope.

When hunting for colleges, I wanted to find a solid Christian university with a Creative Writing major. At the time, that didn't exist. But I fell in love with the University of Northwestern and decided to try for a Communications major.

That lasted for a whopping semester before I felt God redirecting me, and I finally acknowledged all the clues that pointed me to becoming a teacher: high-school electives in mentoring at the nearby elementary school, summers spent teaching in the English Language Learner program, my first college job at the Child Development Center. Not to mention all the people who had told me along the way that I should be a teacher.

I laid down my dream of being an author and embraced the joy of wiping noses, singing phonics songs, and creating science experiments. I seemed to be good at it and I mostly enjoyed it. So, this is what I'm supposed to do, right?

Years passed and I found myself as a missionary stay-at-home mom, which is its own kind of superhero. I got to pair all my child development knowledge with my calling to live among the unreached. I guess *this* is what I'm meant to do. But there was still a stirring—a deep longing—beneath the surface that I couldn't quite identify.

And then I started writing again. Almost out of necessity, I wrote my story of life in Alaska and God met me on those pages. He restored my hope in the power of words and I dared to believe again that maybe, just maybe, I'm designed to do *this*.

A few years ago, when we *happened* to be visiting Minnesota, there *happened* to be a Christian writer's conference at my alma mater. I went. I loved it. Sure, I wanted some incredible connection that would lead to instant publication, but I left with something better.

After the conference finished, I sat at a picnic table overlooking Lake Johanna on the fringe of the campus. I had sat and prayed and walked and wept and studied by these waters many times before, some fifteen years prior. And as He had done so many times before, Jesus met me there.

In a scene only I could see, I watched Him as he tenderly placed a wrapped bundle before me.

"What is it?" I asked.

"Something you gave me long ago that I'm returning to you."

I looked at Him, unsure if I should open it or not. But His smile reassured me, and my fingers flew at the knot. I peered inside, almost afraid to touch something so beautiful.

"This was really mine?" I scarcely recognized my dream, its form fluid and shimmering, a life of its own.

"I've been working on it while it's been in my care. Adding to it with both your pain and your joy. Polishing it with your maturity. Wrapping it in my love. Thanks for letting me watch over it for you. But now it's time for you to open it. Use it. Let it breathe."

Tears of gratitude dripped onto my stack of conference notes. Lake Johanna glistened before me; Naz Hall towered behind me. It was here I laid my dream down and here He gave it back.

And I think—no, I know—that nothing surrendered in obedience to the Lord is ever discarded. Nothing laid at His feet in worship is ever wasted. If he bottles every one of our tears, then he certainly keeps every one of our dreams.

I suspect if you're reading this, you've laid down a dream or two at Jesus's feet. Some may have been born of worldly desires that needed to be replaced by eternal hopes, like the dream of having a beautiful suburban home near an amazing school with a boat tucked in the three-car garage. Maybe that dream is now replaced with living in a high-rise apartment in a crowded Asian city near the university where your daytime students come over for nighttime Bible studies. Yes, some dreams need a good dose of holy refinement.

But then there are those deep dreams. The ones that you've dared to imagine on and off over the years, but they've never come to fruition. The ones that seem to come from your very bones and never quite leave, no matter the season or how you try to convince yourself otherwise. What do we do with those dreams?

If my experience is any indication, we leave them right where they first started—in God's hands. We say "Father, I can't shake the desire to be an author. A parent. A worship leader. An evangelist. An artist. A psychologist. An entrepreneur. A gardener. But I don't see a way right now. Your calling and leading are taking me somewhere else. I don't understand it. I'm not even sure I like it, but I trust you. So, here's my dream—the dream that you gave me. I'm laying it back at your feet, and I want you to hold it for me. Please return it if—when it's time."

It's not only me, though. I think of Moses, who ached so badly for justice for the Israelites that he murdered an Egyptian in his zeal, then had to wait as a shepherd for 40 years before God returned his dream to him to be a deliverer for his people. And there's Abraham, longing for the child of promise and the dream of descendants who, when he finally received a son, was asked by God to sacrifice

Isaac on an altar. God, as you well know, stopped him and returned his dream, his very heart, to his embrace. Then there's Joseph. Job. Even the disciples, who had to lay down their dream of seeing God's kingdom come through freedom from Roman oppression. That dream went to the tomb with Jesus.

But just as their dream felt dead and crushed, like Jesus's very body, it rose again with Him in a transformed glory they had never imagined. The kingdom of heaven at hand!

God doesn't do death. Resurrection, yes. But death, no. The only thing that truly dies is death itself.

Hear this reminder one more time, dear ones: nothing surrendered in obedience to the Lord is ever discarded. Nothing laid at His feet in worship is ever wasted. If he bottles every one of our tears, then he certainly keeps every one of our dreams.

You keep track of all my sorrows. You have
collected all my tears in your bottle. You have
recorded each one in your book. (Psalm 56:8 NLT)

Catch the Rain

Here you are invited to open your heart in the presence of Jesus. Please choose *1 or 2 reflection responses* that you are drawn to. You can take time for this. You are worth it.

- Do you have a deep, unfulfilled dream? Recall when you first became aware of that dream. Does it feel like something God gave to you? Do you tend to think of it as dead or as held by Jesus?

- Prayerfully imagine your dreams in Jesus's hands. What is His expression? How does He handle them? What does He say to you about them?

- Joseph has one of the most detailed life accounts in the Bible. Spend time in his story, Genesis 37–45, and notice how God first gave Joseph his dreams, kept his dreams, and finally brought those dreams to life.

- Create a physical representation of your deepest dream. Put it somewhere that symbolizes surrender to you. Trust God to nurture it while you wait.

The Table is Set

WHEN MY SOUL IS PARCHED AND I need a cool drink, if not a complete drenching, there is one place that never fails me. That place, as you may have guessed, is God's Word. If I walk away from it as thirsty as I arrived, it's usually because I'm rushing. The Spirit, however, is never in a hurry and is always speaking through the Bible.

"For the word of God is alive and active. Sharper than any double-edged sword, it penetrates even to dividing soul and spirit, joints and marrow; it judges the thoughts and attitudes of the heart" (Hebrews 4:12).

I'm preaching to the choir, no doubt. You've probably been reading and even teaching the Bible for years. But there is a great chasm between dissecting and drinking the Word of God.

There's a fancy Latin name for drinking deeply from scripture. It's called *lectio divina*, which means sacred reading, inspired understanding, Holy Spirit-touched scripture meditation. It's a way of letting the Word read you.

In *Life with God*, Richard Foster emphasizes that "[t]here is a vast difference between reading the surface of the biblical text and encountering the God who divinely superintended its delivery into our hands—the God who proclaims to you and to me, 'I am with you. . . will you be with Me?'"[1]

I don't know about you, but I am not always so good at slowing down in my scripture reading and being *with* God. I love to engage my intellect and I get unreasonably excited over new insights from word studies and the historical background of the Bible. Or, more commonly, I just have a lot to do after my "quiet time." I investigate with my mind or I rush through the text, either way, missing a transformative encounter with the Spirit.

"Remember, the point is to go deep, not wide. . . . Complicated is not the same as deep. New is not the same as deep. Interesting is not the same as deep. To go deep is to go in to the HEART of the matter and to allow the matter to go deep in to the HEART," says Brian K. Rice.[2]

Lectio divina helps me get into the heart of scripture and allow it to go deep into my heart. It is the practice of feasting and drinking at God's table. And it is a beautiful reminder that God is forever and always pursuing an intimate relationship with us. He is always speaking.

Do you remember when I told you about the time I failed miserably at waking up early in order to study through the Bible in one year? I desperately wanted a transforming touch from the Lord, and I knew the place to go was His Word, but the only way I knew to engage with it was through my mind. At the time, my body was exhausted and my emotions constantly on edge. Feeding my mind was not enough.

Jesus gave me discernment to be more gentle with my body and more gracious with my soul by switching my Bible reading time to the afternoon and shortening the amounts I read. That helped some. But it wasn't until about a year later when I was introduced to the slow, intentional, prayerful reading of scripture that I really found what I was after—peace, restoration, and heart change.

There is no balm for the soul like the voice of God.

The astounding part is, He *wants* to speak to me. He *longs* to embrace me. He *intentionally* pursues me, guides me, and prepares more goodness for me to feast upon in His presence than I can possibly consume.

Come, all you who are thirsty,
*   come to the waters;*
and you who have no money,
*   come, buy and eat!*
Come, buy wine and milk
*   without money and without cost.*
Why spend money on what is not bread,
*   and your labor on what does not satisfy?*
Listen, listen to me, and eat what is good,
*   and you will delight in the richest of fare.*
Give ear and come to me;
*   listen, that you may live.* (Isaiah 55:1–3)

The table is set. The feast is free. Your only response is to come and listen.

CATCH THE RAIN

As you respond to this invitation, here are some tools to help you listen to scripture in a new way.

First, get still and quiet. This is a practice in and of itself in our modern world of busy schedules and instant gratification. You might find it helpful to light a candle and just watch the flame, close your eyes and listen to an instrumental song, or repeat a gentle breath prayer, such as "Speak, Lord; your child is listening." Try to stay in the stillness for two to five minutes.

Second, read a small passage of scripture. Often, just a verse or two will do. If you want to try it now, Isaiah 55 above would be a lovely selection. Read the passage at least three times. First, familiarize yourself, next, pay attention to what it stirs within you, and last, read it one more time in search of what the Spirit is highlighting to you.

Third, reflect on and process what resonated with you from the text. Write it down. Ponder its connection to your day, your past, your future musings. You might enjoy drawing one word that stood out to you in bold letters or artful script. Sit with what stirred you.

Fourth, talk to God about it. This should be a two-way conversation. You might ask Him why a certain phrase made you feel excited or sad or confused. Then listen for His response. You might want to give Him thanks or praise. Simply talk with Him.

Fifth, just breathe and rest. Enjoy this time spent with Jesus. Savor His nearness and love. Store up His words in your heart. Drink deeply.

Sixth, take it all with you. Spending time with our Father, hearing the voice of Christ, and feeling the comfort of the Spirit will always mark us. We leave this time changed, transformed just a bit more into the image of Christ. Whatever He spoke to you from His Word, act on it immediately and keep it in your mind throughout the day.

Another time, another day, another season of your soul, you can return to the text to uncover its original meaning and historical context. You can find themes and root words and models for evangelism. But for now, O weary soul, take time to be personally refreshed and washed in the Word. All the rest will be that much richer because of it.

> The Lord is my shepherd, I lack nothing.
>> He makes me lie down in green pastures,
> he leads me beside quiet waters,
>> he refreshes my soul.
> He guides me along the right paths
>> for his name's sake.
>> Even though I walk through the darkest valley,
>> I will fear no evil, for you are with me;
>> your rod and your staff,
> they comfort me.

You prepare a table before me
in the presence of my enemies.
You anoint my head with oil;
my cup overflows.
Surely your goodness and love will follow me
      all the days of my life,
and I will dwell in the house of the Lord
forever. (Psalm 23)

The table is set. Will you come?

Catch the Rain

Here you are invited to open your heart in the presence of Jesus. Please choose *1 or 2 reflection responses* that you are drawn to. You can take time for this. You are worth it.

- What has Bible reading looked like for you recently? Rushed or slow? To study or to hear God? Dry or rich? Do you desire more from it?

- Practice *lectio divina* again with a passage of your choosing.
  1. Get still
  2. Read it three times slowly, listening to the Spirit
  3. Reflect
  4. Pray
  5. Savor and rest
  6. Take it with you

- Share how God is speaking to you from His Word with a friend and ask them about their Bible reading practices and if/how they're hearing the Spirit through scripture. Try *lectio divina* together. It's incredible to see how personally we each encounter God through the Bible.

Part 6
HINENI

Then I heard the voice of the Lord saying,
"Whom shall I send? And who will go for us?"
And I said, "Here am I. Send me!"

— Isaiah 6:8

There is a powerful word in Hebrew that sums up
three words in English. The word is Hineni (הנני), which
means "Here I am!" But you've got to watch out how you
say it, because it is a way of expressing total readiness to
give oneself – it's an offer of total availability.

— One For Israel, "Hineni": Here I Am. Send Me! [1]

KEY STEP:
PERSEVERE REALISTICALLY

We've made it to Part Six. I sincerely hope that you've found my stories relatable and my suggestions for growth helpful. But, as wonderful as a book can be, it doesn't offer the human connection and support that we all need. For this final step, I'd like to suggest the practice of *confession.*

By confession, I simply mean that you place yourself in a community that will keep you accountable and make sure you have at least one friend you can be completely honest with. We persevere, yes, but we do it realistically knowing that we are fallible, and we need help every step of the way. Here are some ideas for practicing confession:

- Start by being completely vulnerable and honest in your journals before the Lord
- Regularly ask God to search your heart
- Talk to a trusted friend about ongoing struggles and plan for a time to meet regularly
- Take opportunities to be prayed for at your local church
- Find a mentor to offer wisdom to you

This is My Yes

THIS BOOK HAS JUST ABOUT caught up to me—to the current page-marker of my heart, my story, my walk with Jesus. I write this final section with a dose of trepidation. What's after this? I don't know yet. But I am learning that the only way forward with Jesus is through my yes to His invitations.

A few weeks ago, I sat across from a friend, a mentor, a big sister, really. The air purifier in her classroom hummed in the background, attempting to keep the hazardously smoky air at healthy levels. Dry season hit hard this year, and the fires—intentional and unintentional— had us all trapped indoors, praying for rain.

"So, where are we with this? Do you still have questions or are you ready for the firehose?" she asked.

I smiled, totally unprepared but certain of one thing. "I'm a 'yes' to this. I'm all in." And for the next hour I reviewed all the details of my new role as Chapel Coordinator at our international school. We talked schedules, teaming, prayer life, improvement plans, past failures to avoid, future hopes and dreams, and the reality of the spiritual battle and weight I had just agreed to.

This isn't a small yes, I realized. *Am I ready?* I wondered. *I'm scared*, I confessed. *Please be my strength and my help in it all*, I prayed.

Throughout these pages I've remembered what it was like to do all the right things for Jesus yet feel far from Him. I've recalled my desperate need to *feel* the love of Christ, to *hear* God's voice, to *know* Him intimately. I've recounted moments of great freedom and discovery and the struggles that wrought them. In the looking back, I see the growth. I have a settled place in God's love that is more secure than ever before. But, at the same time, I'm still there—still far and desperate and struggling.

But isn't that the point? To think I've arrived is to return to where I began. I'm nowhere near the end of getting to know my infinite God. And that, my friend, is a very good thing.

Let me pause to remind you: No two journeys are the same. There are similarities, yes. And I certainly hope my story has been relatable so that you don't feel alone in your weariness. But I have condensed into the pages of this book what took me about five years to live out. It takes time, practice, and perseverance to develop new ways of knowing and being with Jesus.

If you find yourself still thinking "I'm not about to tell God 'Here I am!' again. That's what got me into this mess to begin with," that's okay. In fact, it's a great place to start a conversation. Wherever you are on your journey, know that Jesus is there with you. Even if you can't see Him because the valley is too dark, He's still there.

Your only job is to learn to trust.

At the outset, trust might not be so hard. We're eager. Excited. Ready for something new. It's in the middle that faith is tested—when you've lost sight of Who called you to begin with, and you're off the map from where you thought you were headed.

The middle is the Israelites, camping in the desert, hungry and thirsty, following a God they barely know toward freedom. But if sand and stones and scorching sun is freedom, then they wonder if they should have followed this God in the first place.

The middle is Elijah under a broom tree, discouraged, disheartened, and depressed. He had just proved through calling down fire from heaven followed by rain that Yahweh, not Baal, was God. But still he was hated and hunted and alone.

The middle is Jesus in the Garden of Gethsemane, sweating blood as He pleaded with His Father. He knew the full extent of the physical and spiritual torture He was about to endure. What person on this planet would willingly subject themselves to such horror?

But we know the endings, don't we? We know that the Israelites eventually entered the Promised Land, becoming caretakers of the very words of the Lord, hosts of His presence, holders of the messianic promises.

175

We know God saw Elijah's weariness and discouragement because He sent an angel to minister to Elijah, then called him away to have a very profound and personal encounter with the I AM—whispering reassurance to Elijah's heart. Elijah went on to finish well. He trained Elisha and rode into glory in a heavenly chariot.

And we know Jesus's obedience. The suffering He endured for the joy set before Him. The glory and victory of the resurrection. The complete authority He holds over death. The hope of His return to make all things new. All this accomplished by, "Not my will, but Yours be done."

Hineni—here I am, Lord.

Or to sum it up in one word: yes.

Those yeses—and the hundreds more chronicled throughout the pages of scripture—made history. They charted a way forward for me and you so we can see that trusting God's plan and His heart is worth it all.

I speak this into a time when much of Western culture treats "yes" lightly. Freedom of choice is king, and respecting others' decisions is queen. It's your right to change your mind, your marriage, even your gender, is it not? We're constantly in search of a better fit. An easier way. But in our fickle yeses, we're running back to Egypt, preferring worldly slavery over bond service to Christ.

Usually, we need to stay in the messy middle. Only then will we make it to victory.

It might not feel like it at the moment, but the only safe yes is a yes to Jesus. A yes to His way, His truth, and His life. Nothing else will satisfy.

And nothing else will hurt quite so much.

Isaiah the prophet told the Lord, "*Hineni!* Here I am! Send me.*" But first, he was purified in the Lord's presence by a burning coal touching his lips. *Ouch.* Then, he was told to speak God's message to people who would be unhearing, unseeing, and unchanged by it. He was given visions of the impending judgment on Judah if they didn't repent. *Ouch.* He preached naked, stripped bare, for three years. He carried the sorrowful picture of Messiah as a rejected, suffering servant. And, as tradition has it, after 40 years of ministry, he was sawn in two by an evil king.[1] *Ouch.*

I wonder if Isaiah ever wished that God would send someone else. I know I have.

But here's the surprising twist that Isaiah discovered: In response to our surrendered yes, God says "Here I am," to us.

Then your light will break forth like the dawn, and your healing will quickly appear; then your righteousness will go before you, and the glory of the Lord will be your rear guard. Then you will call, and the Lord will answer; you will cry for help, and he will say: Here am I. (Isaiah 58:8–9)

Do you hear God's ready response? "Here I am," he says, running toward us, ready to wrap us in His own robe of light, healing, righteousness, and glory.

So, what preceded his welcoming embrace? What does the "then" of verse 8 refer to?

Setting the oppressed free. Feeding the hungry. Sheltering the homeless. Those are some big yeses. They're the yes of the prodigal returning home, recognizing his own oppression, hunger, and homelessness. And out of the Father's lavish love and abundant supply, he gives to others as he has been given.

Verse 10 follows this up with another call to "spend [our]selves on behalf of the hungry and satisfy the needs of the oppressed." But the next verse adds even more fullness to God's promised response.

...then your light will rise in the darkness, and your night will become like the noonday. The Lord will guide you always; he will satisfy your needs in a sun-scorched land and will strengthen your frame. You will be like a well-watered garden, like a spring whose waters never fail. (Isaiah 58:11)

I notice a distinctly repeated phrase in both our mission and God's response: "satisfy the/your needs." If you say yes to satisfying the needs of others, then your Father will say yes to satisfying your own needs. Because what He gives you when you say, "Here I am," is Himself. Fully. Unreserved. He's all in. And He is enough.

"Yes" might lead you to the wilderness. "Yes" might disrupt your comfort. "Yes" might cause rejection or even persecution. But "yes" is the only path home.

What is God asking you to do today? It might be to serve, give, love, or die to yourself. But it also might be to simply lean on His chest and rest. Isaiah 58 ends with one more if/then promise:

> *...if you call the Sabbath a delight and the Lord's holy day honorable, and if you honor it by not going your own way and not doing as you please or speaking idle words, then you will find your joy in the Lord, and I will cause you to ride in triumph on the heights of the land and to feast on the inheritance of your father Jacob.* (Isaiah 58:13)

Delight in His gift of rest, and you will find that your joy always has been, and always will be, the Lord himself. Like a gentle father or a comforting mother, God is holding you, saying, "I'm here. I'm right here."

You're not the only one saying "yes."

Catch the Rain

Here you are invited to open your heart in the presence of Jesus. Please choose *1 or 2 reflection responses* that you are drawn to. You can take time for this. You are worth it.

- How does the idea of saying "Yes! Here I am" to God make you feel? Journal about those feelings and what you think is causing them.

- Reflect on other biblical stories where people said *hineni* to God: Abraham (Gen. 22), Jacob (Gen. 46:1–7), Moses (Ex. 3:1–5), Samuel (1 Sam. 3:1–10), and Ananias (Acts 9:1–19).

- Practice openness to God by beginning each day with the simple prayer, "Here I am, Lord." End each day by reflecting on the ways you said yes to God and how He responded with His presence.

- Are you in the messy middle of a "yes" to God? What did you envision when He first called you? How do you still hope it will play out? Can you discern God's nearness even if nothing looks like you thought it would?

His Kingdom, Not Mine

LITTLE FINGERS GRIPPED THE BACK of the large black office chair, curious eyes and a small nose peeking above them. My heart stopped at the sight. I thought we were being directed to a room where we would meet with our social worker; I hadn't expected to turn the corner and see him. A stranger. My son.

Tears pricked at my eyes as over six years of prayers stared back at me, the flesh and bones of a miracle.

Getting here had not been easy. Paperwork, trainings, years of silence while we waited to be matched, updated documents because of the delay, challenging phone conversations in Thai which I only partially understood, and even a rescheduling of this first meeting because Troy got COVID—all a headache and a hassle. But none of that compared to the heart-work that God wrestled me through along the way.

This—adoption—a journey of open-handed surrender like none other.

Before marriage, I felt a burden for underprivileged and forgotten kids. I wanted to help them someway, somehow. And I believed that I would. Into young adulthood, I watched multiple friends struggle with the grief of infertility and miscarriage. I admired their perseverance in

181

finding a way to build a biological family, but I knew that I would, if necessary, choose adoption over extreme medical intervention.

Then, an easy pregnancy. A beautiful birth. A perfect baby boy was placed in my arms. I held Chanan Isaiah, whose name means gracious salvation of Yahweh, and every part of my torn and weary body screamed a fierce love for him. I studied his big, dark eyes, his pink lips, his tiny fingernails, and his round belly with the protruding cord nub where my life had nurtured his for nine months, and I murmured a thanks to God for this incredible human. I loved him completely. Then with my next heartbeat, a thought: *No child should ever grow up without knowing the all-encompassing love of a mother.*

Even there, in that most sacred of moments, God was writing adoption into my heart.

Just over two years later, my beautiful baby girl was born. She was, and is, a perfect gift of joy, my Rinnah Jeannette. My hands and heart were full.

Six months after her birth, we moved to Thailand and muddled our way through culture shock and transition stress. Some days felt nearly unbearable. But even then, a question lingered. Were we still willing to adopt?

We walked with several families through their adoption journeys and saw firsthand that it was an arduous and often exhausting process. One family struggled so deeply with their child's Reactive Attachment Disorder that they relinquished the adoption and sent their little girl on to a new family. Heartbreak upon heartbreak.

I honestly didn't know if I could do it. If I could hold the brokenness, like shards of shattered pottery, to my chest. I could have brushed the burden aside; I never felt that God was making me. But even on my worst of days, I understood adoption as an invitation to join the Father in His redemptive work. He gave of Himself, was ripped wide open, to birth His children. I had done the same physically, and, I knew, I would choose to do the same emotionally.

Time and again I doubted, was tossed in the waves. And time and again I came back to trust. I had everything I wanted in my little kingdom, but then His Spirit would remind me whose kingdom I was called to build.

To join God's kingdom work is to join an upside-down kingdom. It's a kingdom where the last—the least of these, like the orphan—are first, where tiny seeds bear eternal fruit, and where sacrificial love triumphs over self-protection. This kingdom is filled with adoptees. You, me, and every other person orphaned by sin and brought home by grace.

The posture of those who belong to this heavenly kingdom is open hands, arms spread wide. It's release and surrender simultaneous with praise and receptivity. It's the intention behind the lyrics of "Nothing I Hold Onto":

"I lean not on my own understanding; my life is in

the hands of the Maker of Heaven. . . I give it all to you, God, trusting that you'll make something beautiful out of me. . . I will climb this mountain with my hands wide open. . . There's nothing I hold onto."[1]

Climbing a mountain with hands wide open does not make sense. If you're climbing a steep slope with loose shale sliding beneath your shoes, you need your hands to help keep your balance and hold on. To climb a mountain with open hands implies a deep trust that you will be caught if you slip. You do not have to support yourself. You are tethered to the One who has climbed this mount before you. All you need to do is follow His trail of blood.

It's counterintuitive. And it's absolute freedom, this open-handed climb, like a child scaling a rock-climbing wall quick as Spiderman due to the harness secured at his waist and the strength of the instructor holding his rope. We climb, we fall, we are caught. We are free to take risks, knowing that it's Love calling us upward and Love giving momentum.

One of the clearest themes throughout my Christian life has been that of surrender. I recall driving home through winding mountain roads as a teenager, contemplating difficult friendships, weighty school assignments, and ever-looming future decisions and plans, and being drawn back to songs and prayers of surrender time and again. Outside, I gripped the steering wheel, scanning the roadside through misted eyes for darting deer, yet inside I spread my palms skyward, closed my eyes, and released my life once again to my Keeper. *I give it all to you, God, trusting that you'll make something beautiful out of me.* In every desire, every decision, every pain—surrender. Trust. Free-fall into Love. An invitation to each of us.

I approached the office chair and the small head with bristling, black hair that peered over it, waved hello with a smile, and sat down to begin again this familiar adventure of motherhood—the one where I love fiercely and spend myself sacrificially for the growth of another. It's a wild and holy place. Disruptive and disquieting to my kingdom, but joyful and enriching to His.

Open hands, open heart, open eyes—I want to see His kingdom come.

Catch the Rain

Here you are invited to open your heart in the presence of Jesus. Please choose *1 or 2 reflection responses* that you are drawn to. You can take time for this. You are worth it.

- Take some quiet moments to consider what you're holding onto. Is there anything you grip out of fear, pride, or tradition? What would being open-handed with that look like, feel like?

- Worship with songs of surrender, such as "Nothing I Hold Onto" by United Pursuit, "I Surrender" by Hillsong, and the hymn "I Surrender All."

- Is there a new risk God is inviting you to take? A way He is asking you to partner with Him in His redemptive work? Journal about any feelings of hesitancy or doubt you have about it. Lay it out honestly before God and ask Him to reply.

- Meditate on Psalm 37, considering the call to trust in, hope in, and delight in the Lord and His promised protection and help.

It's Me Again

I HANDED THE MID-TERM EXAM to my professor, feeling accomplished and proud of the four pages I'd just hand-written in Spanish about several Latino authors of the past. He took the test but didn't return my smile. Figuring he was in one of his typical, serious moods, I turned for the door and the Spring Break mission trip that began in just two days. But before I could take a step, he called me back.

"May I please see your hand." Though quietly spoken in a thick accent, the professor had gotten the attention of the remaining students, and I could feel their curious eyes watching us.

Heat rushed up my neck as I opened my left palm before him. The same palm on which were written initials and years of birth and death. My language-wired brain could remember the words, but not the numbers, so I'd justified writing the required dates on my hand. And I'd been caught.

The professor frowned. "Meet me in my office at 4pm."

I nodded dumbly. *What have I done?*

"And read the handbook policy on cheating before you come in," he added, as I stumbled out of the room.

The next 24 hours are a blurred memory compared to the poignant horror of those first few moments of exposure. I know I called my mom. I sobbed. I read the handbook and discovered that any act of cheating on an exam warranted a failed course. I prayed for mercy. I told Troy, who had himself once cheated on an assignment in high school and had at least a little empathy. I wept more. I met with my disappointed professor and gave him my pathetic explanation. He conceded that if I continued to do my work to the best of my ability, he might give me a D-. I called my mom again. I packed for my trip to Tijuana, feeling like the scum of the earth who should in no way be allowed to build sidewalks at an orphanage. And eventually I accepted my fate: I would put full effort into this, my hardest class, all for the hopeful reward of a measly D-. Not an easy task for someone who is used to straight As.

Did I learn from my mistake? You can be sure I never handed in an exam with the same hand I wrote answers on again. Rookie mistake. No, in seriousness, I never cheated again. At least not on a college exam.

This whole drama played out during my freshman year of college. That was a hard year. An undoing year. A year of discovering my belovedness in Christ without the usual awards, pats on the back, and hometown feature newspaper articles I had become used to. I was just little-fish-in-a-big-pond me.

To comfort my dying ego (or perhaps to fully bury it), God drew me to Psalm 139. There, I was reminded of how intimately God knew me, how specifically He created me, how intentionally He pursued me, and how purposefully He refined me. For most of that year, I prayed this Psalm daily, ending sincerely with these final verses:

> *Search me, God, and know my heart; test me and know my anxious thoughts. See if there is any offensive way in me, and lead me in the way everlasting.* (Psalm 139:23–24)

I think there was a direct correlation between my prayers for God to know my heart, test me, and point out my offensive ways, and the exposure of my cheating on that Spanish mid-term. It's not that I was a compulsive cheater. I'd always studied hard and completed assignments as asked. Cheating wasn't my problem. Pride was. Seeking man's praise was. Propping my identity up on my accomplishments was.

Still is.

I didn't weep over disappointing my professor or realizing I'd done something wrong; I wept out of shame that I'd been caught, embarrassed, and would have to work just as hard for absolutely no reward. Is there any offensive way in me? Yes. A thousand times, yes. And did it hurt that God exposed it? Excruciatingly so. But to what end did He reveal this gunk in my soul? So He could lead me in the everlasting way of life.

The alternative? Death. Death of connection. Death of relationships. Death of all He has made me to be. Sin is our present reality, and its wounds always fester.

Only the light of the Spirit exposes our darkness in a way that brings life and health and peace.

The sinful bent of each personality doesn't disappear overnight. Writing books is a battleground for me where I must diligently guard against my desire for affirmation from man and worth from my works. Parenting has unearthed landmines of selfishness, impatience, and rage in me. Living abroad has exposed unhealthy self-reliance, and joining a transient community of expats has revealed guardedness in my soul.

In short, life tests us. We sin, shed a layer of brokenness, and are tested again, revealing a deeper layer to it all. So the cycle continues. We are never past our need for healing from the Lord. At least, not this side of heaven.

As we learn to persevere realistically, to trust Jesus with another "yes," and to keep moving further into His love, we also must learn to continually let God search us.

Not long after my deeply refining freshman year, I was asked to share at my home church. Naturally, I chose Psalm 139. Most of the chapter is delightful, encouraging, and hopeful. Then David drops this right before the ending prayer:

If only you, God, would slay the wicked! Away from me, you who are bloodthirsty! They speak of you with evil intent; your adversaries misuse your name. Do I not hate those who hate you, Lord, and abhor those who are in rebellion against you? I have nothing but hatred for them; I count them my enemies. (Psalm 139:19–22)

I wrestled with this text, considering whether to even acknowledge its presence within the Psalm. But it has a place there, just as it has a place in my own life.

As the rest of the Psalm focuses on God's intimate knowledge of David, we can conclude that this part does, as well. Yes, he faced literal, bloodthirsty men. But perhaps here he is also thinking of himself, longing to hate the sin and deceit within his own soul.

David, of all people, knew the destructive power of sin. And he hated it. Just as God hates sin not only because it disgusts or offends Him, but also because it destroys those He loves. And so, David concludes this song with a prayer for God to search him, to know him, and even to test him. He doesn't want any semblance of sin going undealt with in his life. And neither should we.

We persevere on this journey with Jesus realistically, knowing that we'll slip up. We'll veer off the path entirely sometimes. But in His goodness, our Guide will show us

191

the error of our ways and get us pointed in the right direction again—on the way of everlasting life.

Catch the Rain

Here you are invited to open your heart in the presence of Jesus. Please choose *1 or 2 reflection responses* that you are drawn to. You can take time for this. You are worth it.

- Try a *lectio divina* on Psalm 139. What stands out to you? Converse with God about it.

- Set up a regular time for reflection and confession. You can use Psalm 139:23–24 to guide your prayer. Write down any sin God reveals, repent to him, and confess it to a trusted friend.

- What are some of the consistent sins you battle? What brings them to the surface in your life? If you're not sure, go over this list prayerfully: pride, lust, greed, laziness, envy, selfishness, gossip, deceit, excessiveness, crude language, idolatry, sexual perversion, hate, divisiveness. . .

- Meditate on Ephesians 5:1–20. What counter activities are suggested for a holy life rather than a sinful life?

Seasonal Growth

I RISE FROM SLUMBER, eyes blinking, emerging into a new day, breathing in the cool dawn. A whispered prayer, a text of scripture—sacrament and sustenance for the rush ahead. I stretch and receive this gift of life.

The children mill around, laughing, arguing, playing, creating. I feed them, the cats, and the fish. Wash the dishes and the laundry. Answer emails. Tasks are being accomplished in the work of the day.

Dinner is on the table as tired, dirty faces gather around. A recap of the day is shared, a final plea for wrestling or basketball answered. One foot in front of the other to finish the day, putting crazy-tired bodies to bed. The fullness of each moment now weighs heavy, and I long to lay myself down.

Finally, sleep. An entering of the grave of bedsheets. Stillness. Slow breathing. A pause on the outside while the inside rejuvenates, heals, folds information from the day into creases of dreams. I await the resurrection of the morning.

Each day is a miniature lapsing of seasons. We move from the spring of waking to the summer of producing to the fall of weariness to the winter of rest. All this exactly as our Creator designed.

It's beautiful in its rhythm that moves from preparation to harvest and back again. Each piece of the day has its place, its purpose and its dependency on the others. How good it is to work hard, accomplishing much, and long for sleep. How pleasant it is to rest well and awake refreshed to a new day.

Yet we often ignore the sanctity of these rhythms, favoring production over sleep or escapism over fruitfulness. It's the same in our spiritual lives.

Not only does your spiritual life move through these agrarian-type seasons (most easily recognized by the Western definition of spring, summer, autumn, and winter), but each one is equally valuable, beautiful and purposeful.

AUTUMN

If your soul is in autumn or winter, the freshness of spring or the fruitfulness of summer might feel impossibly far away. However, if you've ever lived in a climate where the flurry of summer's activity slows into the crisp release of fall, you know that autumn carries a distinct and welcome beauty.

Autumn typically whispers its way into our lives with a chilling wind here, an early frost there. We still dance in the sunshine, kicking up crimson leaves, but the days grow shorter and with them our enthusiasm. There is much to be done before winter, and autumn is the season of endurance through harvest, perseverance through in-gathering. In other words, in fall, we reap what we sow.[1]

The spiritual season of autumn might feel like the burden of carrying to completion what was once done with excitement. It might be anticipating a final product; the urgency of finishing a task well; a growing weariness that craves deep rest. And it often includes letting go and feeling the first icy touch of grief.

WINTER

Nature demonstrates that a season of dormancy is necessary for the growth and fruitfulness of a plant. Whether that season is laden with snow or barren of rain, the effect is the same, and a forced rest will happen before any fruit is born.

You've likely heard the quip that if you don't rest physically, your body will eventually force you to. Could this be true spiritually, as well? God's model of Sabbath rest would suggest so as we see that the Israelites' time in exile directly related to the number of years they failed to let the ground rest (see Leviticus 26:34–35).

Sometimes we need to *choose* to winter after a heavy harvest. Other times, however, something tragic ices the landscape of our souls without warning. There's no choosing about it. The blizzard is upon us and we can only hold onto the rope tied to the barn while we blindly stumble toward shelter.

A winter of the soul might look like a craving for still-ness and silence; a loss of felt connection with God; the deep grief of losing a loved one, a dream, a home, stabil-ity, or health; lack of motivation to pray or passionless prayers; the stalled emptiness of waiting on a critical life change over which you have little control; or a ministry devoid of fruit despite your efforts.

While all this barren silence might sound frightening, know that deep work is going on beneath the surface dur-ing winter. Often, God has recently done some serious renovation in your heart and now it's settling in, taking root. In this season you don't need to press the Lord for a new word or a fresh dose of passion; rather you can lean into the last thing He told you and rest in the stillness. The deeper your quiet, the more fruitful your spring.

SPRING

In Alaska, there's an incredible phenomenon called "breakup." The thick river ice, once a highway for snow-mobiles, literally breaks up and flips completely over to begin its journey to the ocean. It's the official signal for the beginning of spring, regardless of the calendar date.

Once, when my wintering soul began its breakup pro-cess, I at first mistook it for a breakdown. And it could have been, but for God. When He starts waking and shak-ing things up inside it can be a painful process, but if we tune into the work His Spirit is doing and join Him in tilling the packed earth of our hearts, new growth will surely follow.

If winter is marked by silence, then spring is marked by noise. Particularly, the voice of the Lord. God is never silent, but in winter He is harder to hear. God calls to you almost audibly in spring. You can resist it or ignore it, telling Him "I like my armchair by the fireplace, thank you very much," but you'll be missing one of the greatest opportunities for personal growth and planting in His kingdom.

Springtime is an invitation from the Lord to sow seeds.

Is God calling to you? Stirring things in your soul and bringing buried longings to the surface? Inviting you to take a tenuous step of faith? Don't miss the invitation to join Him in springtime renewal, no matter how messy the whole digging and planting process might be.

SUMMER

Summer brings to mind sun-splattered memories of water play, mountain hikes, and baskets full of berries. It's family, reconnecting with old friends, catching up on outside projects, and fingers sticky with perfectly toasted marshmallow goo. It's more spontaneous, more relaxed, and yet more full than the other seasons.

What words and images do you associate with summer? Perhaps *freedom. Abundance. Laughter.*

Connection. Celebration. Or maybe *transition. Goodbye. Exploration. Sweat. Maintenance.*

A spiritual summer is a season of plenty—growth comes easily, productivity naturally. Your connection with God feels enjoyable and you generally feel supported by others, as well. You're involved in meaningful ministry where God is at work around you. You're up for the challenge of accomplishing whatever He has called you to. Hospitality might even come easily, and God's unmerited grace and lavish kindness are often on your lips—so much so that you feel a tad bit guilty about the ease and joy of your life whenever a friend shares her struggles with you.

Let's wrestle with that last one. *Should* we feel guilty for being in a season of relative abundance, peace, or success?

I'm not really a fan of the trite saying that everyone is either in a trial, coming out of a trial, or heading into a trial, but I suppose there's truth to it. Life is hard on this sin-broken planet, and it won't be perfect until Jesus makes all things new. However, our God created a baby's laughter, hedgehogs, and raspberries. He is a God of joy, and being fully awake to and appreciative of the things that are rich with it brings Him glory.

Enjoy your summer. Give thanks in it and for it. And, by all means, hold it gently as a gift, knowing that you've done nothing to deserve it.

For everything there is a season. Will these seasons look the same the next time around? Definitely not. Does your spiritual rhythm match mine? Very unlikely. Might this spring or summer be touched by the icy hand of winter like a North Idaho snow on the fourth of July? Probably.

These things are rarely a perfect circle. Life is wobbly and haphazard, but when we pull back a step or two, we can often see an overlay of the seasons, and, somehow, that perspective can help everything feel more *right*. More purposeful. More beautiful, wherever you are.

Western culture may value times of fruitfulness over stillness, but not so in Kingdom culture. Each season is necessary and intentional. Be patient with the process and God will help you see his hand in every season.

Mark Buchanan confesses, "I had worked for many years with rickety logic: religious busyness is the same thing as spiritual maturity. The more you do, the more you love Jesus. . . But the flaws in this equation began to show. I noticed that busyness bruises, stunts, rots fruit as much as grows it. And then I saw it, hidden in plain sight: if we are to bear much fruit—if that's the goal of the Christian life—then the best model for spiritual maturity is seasons. Fruit grows in seasons, and all seasons are necessary for growing it. And seasons are as much about what is not happening as what is. It has as much to do with inactivity as with activity, waiting as with working, barrenness as with abundance, dormancy as with vitality.

For everything there is a season."[2]

Catch the Rain

Here you are invited to open your heart in the presence of Jesus. Please choose *1 or 2 reflection responses* that you are drawn to. You can take time for this. You are worth it.

- What season do you identify most closely with right now? The freshness and hope of spring, the playfulness and bounty of summer, the perseverance and sorrow of autumn, or the stillness and waiting of winter?

- Meditate on Ecclesiastes 3:1–14. What stands out to you?

- Expectations play a big role in contentment. Journal about expectations that have been met and not met from the past week or month. If most of your expectations have not been met, you could be resisting your season. Ask God to give you His expectations for this season of your soul.

- Create something to represent and honor the four seasons as a way to remember the significance and beauty of each. (This could be a photo col-

lage, painting, poem, word art, quilt, bouquet, or
lock screen.

Roots

I SAT IN THE SHADE of the massive tree, enjoying her branches that canopied over me and the shimmers of sunlight filtering through her dainty leaves. She was a beauty. Her strong trunk looked like five regular-sized trees joined at the waist. Her full umbrella was decorated with puffs of wispy, pink flowers reminiscent of something from a Dr. Seuss book.

I want to be like this tree, I thought (a common musing for my mind). Steady. Graceful. Unmoved by the storms and unharmed by the seasons. A haven of rest and shelter.

A whisper stirred in my soul: *Consider the roots.*

The span of her branches must have reached at least 70 feet across. The roots even wider. If her root system were too shallow or narrow, she would topple and die, unable to support the breadth of her wings.

Consider the roots. What I experienced above ground as glory and shelter was only possible by the unseen stability beneath. She was tethered by her roots. Nourished by her roots. Stabilized by her roots. If I want to be a tree like that, I must first grow roots that sink deep into rich, well-watered soil.

I later discovered that this tree I so admired, the *samanea saman*, is most commonly referred to as the rain tree.[1] And I smiled.

My tree-pondering happened at a riverside resort while I retreated for a night and a day to be alone with Jesus. Regular retreats have become one tendril of my root system, anchoring me into focused times of stillness and reflection.

Other root-branches grow through worship, Bible reading, prayer walks, soul talks with friends, journaling, confession, reading or listening to excellent teaching, scripture memorization, Sabbath, fasting, and giving thanks. As I practice these things, I'm nourished in the soil of Christ's love. Some are my anchors—tap roots of sorts—that I depend on day in and day out. Others are still young and tender, thickening and developing with time, not sustaining me quite yet.

Consider the roots. What people see in me, receive from me, is kept alive only because of what they don't see—the hidden inner world of a life rooted in Christ. Jesus always has been, and always will be, the source of it all.

I pray that out of his glorious riches he may strengthen you with power through his Spirit in your inner being, so that Christ may dwell in your hearts through faith. And I pray that you, being rooted and established in love, may have power,

together with all the Lord's holy people, to grasp
how wide and long and high and deep is the love
of Christ, and to know this love that surpasses
knowledge—that you may be filled to the measure
of all the fullness of God. (Ephesians 3:17–19)

It's one of my favorite Pauline prayers. Rooted and established in love. And Paul prays it not just for the church at Ephesus, he prays it for you, as well: "all the Lord's holy people." We are strengthened through the indwelling Spirit of Christ as He testifies to our hearts that we belong to Love. A love so deep and wide and long and high that we can never, not even throughout the span of eternity, reach its end. This is a love you can grasp onto, although you can't grasp it intellectually. It's a love you can be filled up with, although you can't measure its fullness.

This love is the soil our roots must grow into. The underground growth, the heart-work, is of absolute importance. We'll topple in the storms without strong roots.

As one pastor of a mega-church confessed after having an affair and resigning from his ministry, "Over the years I did not do an adequate job of protecting my own spirit, refilling my own soul and reaching out for the readily available help that is available. When you lead out of an empty place, you make choices that have real and painful consequences."[2]

Caring for our roots protects us from those empty places and their painful consequences. So what does root-care look like? I'd dare to say it looks a lot like the practices already offered throughout these pages: listening to the state of your soul and the voice of the Lord; creating safe spaces for healing and restoration; getting deeply personal with God; bringing your whole self into His consuming love; letting God fight for you as you trust His power and authority; and persevering realistically through every season of your soul.

There's more, much more, that can be done to tend your roots, and this framework is only one way to understand it. But it's a good place to start. Because don't we all want to be the tree of Jeremiah 17?

But blessed is the one who trusts in the Lord, whose confidence is in him. They will be like a tree planted by the water that sends out its roots by the stream. It does not fear when heat comes; its leaves are always green. It has no worries in a year of drought and never fails to bear fruit. (Jeremiah 17:7–8)

We love that oft-quoted inspiration, but just before that section, a warning:

Cursed is the one who trusts in man, who draws strength from mere flesh and whose heart turns

away from the Lord. That person will be like a
bush in the wastelands; they will not see prosperi-
ty when it comes. They will dwell in the parched
places of the desert, in a salt land where no one
lives. (Jeremiah 17:5–6)

Trusting in your own strength leads to a barren desert.
Trusting in the Lord's, to confident fruitfulness.

That's why we have to return, again and again, to the
practices that ground us in Christ's love. The temptation
to trust the flesh is ever-present. It's the easiest sin to fall
into. I do it every day. Which is why I must repent every
day and choose Jesus again.

In my choosing, in my practice of habits that help me
abide, I need to remember that this whole thing is more
like a dance than a march. I'm not soldiering on, obeying
orders to "do this, do that!" I'm following the lead of my
Lover as He invites me to draw close and move in rhythm
with His grace. It's invitation, not obligation. He knows
what my soul needs, and, ultimately, I trust Him, not any
practice, to hold me. At the same time, however, I find
that Jesus gives me practical activities that help me focus
on Him and keep in step. He's showing me the dance
moves.

Even trusting in my own self-discipline or daily
rhythms can lead me away from the heart of God. So, I
ask you to hold two paradoxical realities: we need structure, form, and rhythm to facilitate our growth in Christ,

and we are not the ones facilitating or enabling this growth—God is. And we get to join Him in this shaping of our hearts.

Now, with that in mind, consider the roots, again.

We're creatures of habit, of addiction, even. We're drawn to what feeds us. We walk the well-worn paths. We tire of decisions and crave simple routine. This can be a detriment, of course, but it can also be a gift.

I've heard it said that it takes twenty-one repetitions to create a new habit and about three months for it to truly become part of your lifestyle. What do you need in the rhythm of your day, week, and month to connect with Jesus? What habit can you create that will become a taproot into His love?

We can remember the advice of our *Lazy Genius* friend, Kendra Adachi, here again: pick one change, not thirty-seven. And I'd like to suggest that you choose a replacement habit, rather than an additional one—replace a time of disconnect or outright disobedience with a practice of connection and trust. Instead of watching that show that feeds worldly desires, go for a walk and talk to God. Instead of stopping for a sugary macchiato on the way to work, spend ten minutes listening to a devotional app.[3] Instead of hopping straight into the to-do list and the expectations of the day, pray through the Lord's prayer or a Psalm before you even get out of bed.

And once you start a new practice with Jesus, be sure to give yourself lots of grace during its formation and lots of time for it to stick.

"An oak tree has only a couple of months of actual growth. . . The rest of the year, the other ten months, are spent solidifying that growth," writes James Bryan Smith, offering another key lesson from the trees.[4]

I went back to visit the giant, 120-year-old rain tree at that lovely riverside resort again today. She was just as magnificent as ever. And this time, I noticed several other rain trees around the property, one leaning out over the river, another whose roots pushed up from the ground, exposing a girth wider than some of the overhead branches. And under and around each tree, the grass flourished.

As it turns out, the rain tree is so named because her delicate leaves, which appear far too small for her gargantuan size, fold up in a downpour, allowing the rain to drench her roots and for life to flourish at her base.

She knows how to catch the rain.

I pray that you do, too. I pray that you will bravely open your arms to the sky in receptive surrender and feel the downpour of His lavish love. May you know that for every step you take toward the Father, He leaps over the mountains toward you. Every feeble "yes" you breathe is answered with a thunderous "Here I am!" And every tear you've cried is caught in a bottle, mixed with His grace, and poured back out on you as life-renewing rain.

Be strong and courageous, dear ones, for we will not always live in the desert, desperate for rain. The River of Life awaits you.

> *Then the angel showed me the river of the water of life, as clear as crystal, flowing from the throne of God and of the Lamb down the middle of the great street of the city. On each side of the river stood the tree of life, bearing twelve crops of fruit, yielding its fruit every month. And the leaves of the tree are for the healing of the nations.* (Revelation 22:1–2)

Catch the Rain

Here you are invited to open your heart in the presence of Jesus. Please choose *1 or 2 reflection responses* that you are drawn to. You can take time for this. You are worth it.

- What are your current habits for prayer, scripture, worship, reflection, and fellowship? Do you desire more consistency or frequency? What is one new habit you would like to create to root you in Jesus's love?

- Search the scriptures for other verses related to trees. This chapter already mentioned Ephesians 3:17–19 and Jeremiah 17:7–8. What else do you discover?

- Spend some time in nature studying trees. Consider the roots. Listen for any other whispers of the Spirit through what He's created.

- What practice has been touched on in this book that you'd like to revisit and make your own? Don't rush on. Find God's invitation to you in this moment and spend as much time in it as you need.

EPILOGUE

MOMENTS ARE MARKED BY memories, and memories are held by images. How has God been meeting you on these pages? What has He emphasized and highlighted in your life? What is stirring in your soul? What image can help you hold onto this moment?

I'd like to invite you to create an Ebenezer, a memorial stone, to remember it by (see 1 Samuel 7:12, Genesis 28:17–19, and Joshua 4:7–9). The journey is far from over, but the Lord has helped us and held us this far. Find a way to capture His mercy in words, picture, melody, décor, or even tattoo. (Remember my defining mark, *shelhebet-Yah*?) If you do, I'd love to hear about it! Just send me an email at author@corellaroberts.com. Here's one of the Ebenezers along my trail:

"Your Voice is Like the Rain"
July 13, 2020

Your voice is like the rain:
Ceaseless.
This blue planet is showered always.

215

CATCH THE RAIN

Persistent.
Myriad droplets from an unending sky, your call.

Nourishing.
You spoke and life began,
carried on by your word poured out.

Powerful.
Coupled with thunder and awe,
nothing you say returns void.

Commanding.
Under your downpour we scatter, cower,
and cover our heads.

Indiscriminate.
Forest and city, rich and poor,
all receive cleansing when you speak.

Exclusive.
This raindrop, right here, touches my cheek alone.

Without it, we shrivel.
Underneath it, we're washed.

Your voice is like the rain,
And I am a dry and thirsty land

Always craving a fresh downpour,
Soaking You into my fragile roots.

I step out from my umbrella,
Drop it like a clattering shield,
And turn my face upward to receive
Your voice like the rain.

CATCH THE RAIN

ACKNOWLEDGMENTS

It's an impossible task to thank everyone who in some way helped with the development of this book.

On the micro level—the specific details, words, and flow—I'm forever grateful to my earliest test readers. Beth (Mom and cheerleader), Kala (wise friend), and Carolyn (beautiful writer), thank you for believing in my words and both softening and sharpening them in needed ways. Nicole O'Meara (editor extraordinaire), thank you for fine tuning this work and for your instant friendship through our unexpected commonalities. And Troy (beloved husband), thank you for creating time for me to write at your own expense, and thank you for pushing me to stay the course when I grew weary.

On the macro level—the lives that shaped mine and the spiritual journey behind this book—thank you to many friends who guided me and grounded me as I searched for a deeper relationship with my Father. Greg & Corinne, you started all this. Brent & Julie, you are living examples of where I want to be with Christ as I grow. Chris and Tanya, you were the best spiritual friends. Cy, Kassie, Inez, and Dr. Geyman, you've each inspired me through your vulnerability and love. And Jesus, You are the Source, the Beginning and the End. Where would I be without you?

For a *free* reflection guide designed to complement this book, or to receive regular encouragement for your spiritual journey through Corella's blog, go to https://corellaroberts.com

To request group discount prices, please contact author@corellaroberts.com .

ABOUT THE AUTHOR

Corella Roberts makes her home in Northern Thailand where she and her husband partner with an international school to "Serve the Servants." They have three full-of-life kids, two biological and one adopted. From tundra to tropics, her life of following Jesus has been nothing less than story worthy, and she loves using her experiences to encourage others to connect deeply with God. You can find her on Facebook, Instagram, or meandering their local produce market in search of mangosteen and lychee fruit.

Notes

INTRODUCTION
[1] You can read about the physical and spiritual wilderness of my experience in Alaska in *Colliding With the Call: When Following God Takes You to the Wilderness.*
[2] Ortberg, J. (2014). *Soul Keeping: Caring for the Most Important Part of You.* Grand Rapids, MI: Zondervan. Chapter 6, "It's The Nature of the Soul to Need".
(This is an incredible book and if you haven't read it, put it on your list now!)
[3] See Psalm 23
[4] Genesis 2:6 and 3:8
[5] See Revelation 21

Part 1: A DRY AND WEARY LAND
[1] Ortberg, J. (2014). *Soul Keeping: Caring for the Most Important Part of You.* Grand Rapids, MI: Zondervan.
[2] https://www.ignatianspirituality.com/ignatian-prayer/the-examen/

WARNING SIGNS
[1] https://www.thisiscalmer.com/blog/5-stages-of-burnout
[2] https://www.soulshepherding.org/pastors-under-stress/

A SPLINTERED SOUL
[1] Robinson, R. (1758). Come Thou Fount of Every Blessing [lyrics]. Retrieved from https://hymnary.org/text/come_thou_fount_of_every_blessing
[2] Comer, J. M. (2019). *The Ruthless Elimination of Hurry: How to Stay Emotionally Healthy and Spiritually Alive in the Chaos of the Modern World.* London: Hodder & Stoughton.

[3] https://www.umcdiscipleship.org/resources/history-of-hymns-come-thou-fount-of-every-blessing

[1] Hebrews 12:2
[2] Batterson, M. (2020). *Whisper: How to Hear the Voice of God*. Colorado Springs: Multnomah.
[3] Willard, D., & Johnson, J. (2012). *Hearing God: Developing a Conversational Relationship with God*. Downers Grove, IL: Formatio.

EYES TO SEE
[1] Shakespeare, W. (n.d.). Speech: "All the World's a Stage" Retrieved February 25, 2021, from https://www.poetryfoundation.org/poems/56966/speech-all-the-worlds-a-stage
[2] Voskamp, A. (2015). *One Thousand Gifts: A Dare to Live Fully Right Where You Are*. Grand Rapids, MI: Zondervan.

FACE YOUR WALL
[1] Gaultiere, B and K. (2021). *Journey of the Soul: A Practical Guide to Emotional and Spiritual Growth* (p. 13). Ada, MI: Revell.
(This is an excellent resource. I highly recommend it.)
[2] The Runner's World Editors. (2023, April 25). *What is "hitting the wall" during a marathon and how can you avoid it?* Runner's World. https://www.runnersworld.com/uk/training/marathon/a774858/how-to-avoid-the-wall-and-cope-if-you-hit-it/
[3] Gaultiere, B and K. (2021). *Journey of the Soul: A Practical Guide to Emotional and Spiritual Growth* (p. 117). Ada, MI: Revell.
[4] See Exodus 14:14
[1] Palmer, P. J. (2009). *A Hidden Wholeness: The Journey Toward an Undivided Life*. John Wiley & Sons.

THE GIFT OF REST
[1] Matthew 28:19

---

[2] Exodus 20:8-9

[3] My favorite book on Sabbath is *The Rest of God: Restoring your Soul by Restoring Sabbath* by Mark Buchanan. It's beautifully written and will help you reframe your Sabbath mindset toward invitation. Another excellent read that includes a significant section on Sabbath is *The Ruthless Elimination of Hurry: How to Stay Emotionally Healthy and Spiritually Alive in the Chaos of the Modern World* by John Mark Comer.

LINES IN PLEASANT PLACES

[1] The author was Shauna Niequist and the book, *Present over Perfect: Leaving Behind Frantic for a Simpler, More Soulful Way of Living.* It's definitely worth reading.

[2] Zephaniah 3:17, "The Lord your God is with you, the Mighty Warrior who saves. He will take great delight in you; in his love he will no longer rebuke you, but will rejoice over you with singing."

[1] Scazzero, P. (2006). *Emotionally Healthy Spirituality: Unleash a Revolution in Your Life in Christ.* Zondervan.

[2] Manning, B. (2015). *Abba's Child: The Cry of the Heart for Intimate Belonging.* NavPress.

I HEAR YOU, FRIEND

[1] Brown, B. (2012). *Daring Greatly: How the Courage to be Vulnerable Transforms the Way we Live, Love, Parent, and Lead.* Baker & Taylor.

[2] Rice, B. (2012). *The Exercises Volume One: Conversations.* Leadership ConneXtions International.

[3] Jennie Allen. (2021, December 3). *Choosing your People.* Jennie Allen. Retrieved May 4, 2022, from https://www.jennieallen.com/blog/choosing-your-people
Jennie writes and speaks both authentically and biblically. She's

a great resource for growing in relationship with Christ and others.

SEEK MY FACE
[1] see Matthew 10:30 and Psalm 139:4

WHO AM I?
[1] Genesis 17:4-5 and 15-16
[2] Genesis 32:28
[3] Numbers 13:16
[4] Matthew 16:18
[5] Acts 4:36

PRACTICING PRESENCE
[1] Lawrence, B. (2009). *The Practice of the Presence of God: Conversations and Letters of Brother Lawrence*. Oneworld.
[2] For more information on the life of Brother Lawrence visit https://www.christianitytoday.com/history/people/innertravelers/brother-lawrence.html
[3] Again, this is Brother Lawrence's writing as collected in *The Practice of the Presence of God*.

59 SACRED LOVEWAYS
[1] *Discover Your Love Language - The 5 Love Languages®*. Discover Your Love Language - The 5 Love Languages®. (n.d.). Retrieved June 30, 2022, from https://5lovelanguages.com/
[2] Thomas, G. (2021). *Sacred Pathways: Nine Ways to Connect with God*. Zondervan.
[3] Revelation 7:9
[4] Romans 11:36
[5] 1 Timothy 1:17

HEART, SOUL, MIND AND STRENGTH
[1] Heuertz, C. L. (2017). *The Sacred Enneagram: Finding Your Unique Path to Spiritual Growth*. Zondervan.

EMBODIED WORSHIP
[1] Kolber, A. (2020). *Try Softer*. Wheaton, IL: Tyndale House Publishers.
[2] Romans 8:22-23
[3] Warren, T. H. (2016). *Liturgy of the Ordinary*. InterVarsity Press.
[4] *11 Natural Ways to Lower Your Cortisol Levels*. Retrieved August 31, 2022 from, https://www.healthline.com/nutrition/ways-to-lower-cortisol
[5] *Benefits of Strenuous Exercise and How to Add it to Your Workout*. Retrieved August 31, 2022 from, https://www.healthline.com/health/strenuous-exercise#benefits

A LIVING TEMPLE
[1] For an overview of Eric Liddell's life go to https://www.ericliddell.org/biography/ or https://www.christianity.com/church/eric-liddell-greater-than-gold-11634861.html
[2] For an excellent and realistic biography on Elisabeth Elliot, please read *Becoming Elisabeth Elliot* by Ellen Vaughn.
[3] There are countless websites and books detailing the life of Mother Teresa. A quick internet search can provide much information.

SYSTEM REBOOT
[1] Adachi, K., & Freeman, E. P. (2021). *The Lazy Genius Way: Embrace What Matters, Ditch What Doesn't, and Get Stuff Done*. Waterbrook Press.
[2] Same as above.
[3] 1 Peter 5:7
[4] Matthew 11:28

A CONSUMING LOVE
[1] I was gifted The Passion Translation. And I love the Song of Songs in it. However, because of the extensive addition of words and interpretation throughout the text, it's a controversial translation. I've chosen to quote scripture from the New Ameri-

can Standard Bible in this chapter to make sure its meaning can be heard by all and that no one is instantly closed off from receiving the truth of it because of the translation used.
[2] *Kisses Sweeter than Wine: Understanding the Song of Songs.* Retrieved November 2, 2022 from, https://www.myjewishlearning.com/article/song-of-songs/

Part 5: NOT ON MY OWN
[1] Lewis, C.S. (2009). *The Lion, The Witch and the Wardrobe.* HarperCollins.

COURAGE, DEAR HEART
[1] Lewis, C.S. (2009). *The Voyage of the Dawn Treader.* HarperCollins.
[2] Revelation 5:5
[3] Acts 2:3
[4] Lewis, C.S. (2015). *The Great Divorce.* HarperOne.
[5] Lewis, C.S. (2009). *Prince Caspian.* HarperCollins.

ULTIMATE AUTHORITY
[1] My Alaska season in a literal and spiritual wilderness is recorded in *Colliding with the Call: When Following God Takes You to the Wilderness.*
[2] Johnson, D.W. (2004). *Discipleship on the Edge: An Expository Journey Through the Book of Revelation.* Regent College Publishing. This is truly an incredible Bible study on Revelation.
[1] Foster, R. J. (2010). *Life with God: Reading the Bible for Spiritual Transformation.* HarperOne.
[2] Rice, B.K. (2012). *The Exercises Volume One: Conversations.* Leadership ConneXtions International.

Part 6: HINENI
[1] Israel, O. F. (2022, October 30). *"Hineni": Here I am. Send me!* ONE FOR ISRAEL Ministry. Retrieved March 23, 2023, from https://www.oneforisrael.org/bible-based-teaching-from-israel/hineni-here-i-am-send-me/

THIS IS MY YES
[1] See Isaiah 6 (vision of the Lord), 8-9 (judgment), 20:1-4 (preaching naked), 53 (suffering servant).

HIS KINGDOM, NOT MINE
[1] Reagan, W., & Pursuit, U. (n.d.). *Nothing I Hold Onto*. Genius. https://genius.com/Will-reagan-and-united-pursuit-nothing-i-hold-onto-lyrics

SEASONAL GROWTH

[1] Galatians 6:6-8
[2] Buchanan, M. (2010). *Spiritual Rhythm: Being with Jesus Every Season of Your Soul*. Zondervan.

ROOTS
[1] Wikimedia Foundation. (2023, May 16). *Samanea Saman*. Wikipedia. https://en.wikipedia.org/wiki/Samanea_saman#Flowers_and_seeds
[2] Lentz, C. (2020, November 6). Instagram. https://www.instagram.com/p/CHONe5ODr9z/?hl=en
[3] There are some great apps out there to facilitate prayer and scripture meditation. A few of my favorites are The Pause app by John Eldredge, Reimagining the Examen, Lectio 365, Pray as You Go, and Inner Room.
[4] Smith, J. B. (2019). *The Good and Beautiful God: Falling in Love with the God Jesus Knows*. IVP, an imprint of InterVarsity Press.